DEPARTMENT STORE

D1611708

PERRY'S

DEPARTMENT STORE

An Importing Simulation

Donna W. Reamy
VIRGINIA COMMONWEALTH UNIVERSITY

Cynthia W. Steele
EVERGREEN ENTERPRISES, INC.

FAIRCHILD PUBLICATIONS, INC.

NEW YORK

EXECUTIVE EDITOR: Olga T. Kontzias
ACQUISITIONS EDITOR: Joseph Miranda
ASSISTANT ACQUISITIONS EDITOR: Jaclyn Bergeron
ART DIRECTOR: Adam B. Bohannon
PRODUCTION MANAGER: Ginger Hillman
SENIOR DEVELOPMENT EDITOR: Amy Zarkos
ASSOCIATE PRODUCTION EDITOR: Beth Cohen
COPY EDITOR: Douglas Puchowski
TEXT DESIGN AND LAYOUT: Sara E. Stemen
COVER DESIGN: Sara E. Stemen
CD-ROM DEVELOPER: Ron Reeves
CD-ROM MANUFACTURER: Rainbow Multimedia

Copyright © 2006 Fairchild Publications, Inc.

All rights reserved. No part of this book covered by the copyright hereon may be reproduced or used in any form or by any means—graphic, electronic, or mechanical, including photocopying, recording, taping, or information storage and retrieval systems—without written permission of the publisher.

LIBRARY OF CONGRESS CATALOG CARD NUMBER: 2005930303

ISBN 10: 1-56367-382-7
ISBN 13: 978-1-56367-382-5
GST R 133004424

PRINTED IN THE UNITED STATES OF AMERICA

TP08, CM01

Contents

Extended Contents

Preface

The logistics of importing apparel and textiles is an area of the fashion industry that seems to have been overlooked when educating students in the field of fashion merchandising. The knowledge and skills of many fashion professionals from various corners of the world is required to design, produce, and import garments. *Perry's Department Store: An Importing Simulation* emphasizes the importance of conducting business in a global arena while simulating retail buyers' responsibility of importing products to the United States.

The text is organized into ten chapters beginning with background information about the fictitious Perry's Department Store located in Fredericksburg, Virginia. You assume the role of a buyer to learn about the dynamics of the global marketplace and simulate the process of importing denim jeans from a foreign country to the United States. There are eight steps to complete the importing process. An accompanying CD-ROM includes additional resources and worksheets that are necessary to complete the simulation.

When buyers work across borders, they need to cultivate an appreciation for other cultures. Understanding value systems, communication levels, and even time zones contribute to a more professional approach to a business situation.

In today's world it is necessary to understand the economic advancement and importance among developed, developing, and less developed countries. It is essential to gain insight regarding the realistic workings of factories, from those with straw floors to those with cement floors, as well as the ethical issues that buyers may face as they begin to source products.

Upon meeting a prospective businessperson, should buyers bow or shake hands? The text addresses social norms in numerous countries around the world, including what is appropriate with regard to gift giving, gender issues, and negotiations.

Globalization has impacted the fashion industry throughout time. A historical perspective on the textile and apparel trade is examined closely, including the Multi-Fiber Agreement and the phaseout of quotas. The text looks at major trade agreements between the United States and various countries as well as basic trade fundamentals.

Buyers must have support and resources available to them. Therefore, a chapter is devoted to resources for importers from government support to trade associations.

It is crucial to understand the factors that determine the cost of producing an article of clothing. A chapter is devoted to costing the garment and includes examples of a cost sheet where categories are broken down by percentages of total cost. This will help show the areas that can be negotiated and those that are fixed.

The impact of 9/11 on the textile and apparel industry cannot be ignored in this textbook. It emphasizes the importance of the Customs-Trade Partnership Against Terrorism tool and the way it can help to speed up the processes of a product clearing U.S. Customs. The logistics of transporting products and the costs involved help students understand the importance of this step in the supply chain.

Having the product on the floor on time is crucial in the fashion industry. One stopping point can be in clearing customs. A chapter focuses on clearing U.S. Customs and the importing processes and procedures for textiles and apparel. It identifies the necessary forms buyers must complete for products to clear U.S. Customs.

Careers in importing are discussed in the last chapter. It covers not only positions within the fashion industry, such as buyer or product developer, but also positions such as a customs agent who specializes in importing textiles and apparel.

An instructor's guide is available to assist faculty who have never been importers. This manual also includes teaching and learning activities as well as a test bank for midterm and final exams.

Acknowledgments

Many people provided information for this simulation. The authors would like to express their gratitude to the following: Nate Herman, International Trade Director, American Apparel and Footwear Association; Teresa Engle, graphic designer and illustrator; Rose Regni, assistant professor, Department of Fashion Design and Merchandising, Virginia Commonwealth University; Karen Guthrie, chair, Department of Fashion Design and Merchandising, Virginia Commonwealth University; Bruce Cahill, copresident, Jaclyn Apparel; Elaine Crossley, vice president, Jaclyn Apparel; Russell Held, marketing director, Virginia Port Authority; Diana Jackson, import specialist, U.S. Customs; Ed Huebbe, manager, Corporate Communications, MOL (America) Inc.; NETD, Ningbo Economic & Technical Development Zone Merchants Bureau, Ningbo, China; Rajnish Khanna, owner, Source One, Bombay, India; Sandeep Manaktala, partner, Cosmique Global, New Delhi, India; Sonali Rastogi, designer, Cosmique Global, New Delhi, India; Fei Qiu, CEO, Evergreen Enterprises, Inc.; Ting Xu, president, Evergreen Enterprises, Inc.; James Xu, vice president, Evergreen Enterprises, Inc.; *WWD*; and Cotton Incorporated.

To the reviewers who examined the text and offered suggestions for its improvement, we are most appreciative. Reviewers included Richard Clodfelter, University of South Carolina; Jan Hathcote, University of Georgia; Richard Hise, Texas A & M University; Cynthia Jasper, University of Wisconsin; Sharon Pate, Illinois State University; and Robyne Williams, North Dakota State University.

Finally, the authors are especially grateful to Olga Kontzias, executive editor, for her direction and assistance in this project. To our senior development editor, Amy Zarkos; associate production editor, Beth Cohen; art director, Adam Bohannon; and the many other people in the production and marketing departments of Fairchild Publications whose efforts and support made this importing simulation possible: the authors owe them their gratitude.

CHAPTER 1

INTRODUCTION
Perry's Background Information

IN THIS CHAPTER, YOU WILL LEARN:

* What a simulation is and how it is used
* The profile of Perry's Department Store's customer base
* The breadth of a buyer's job in the role of importing

This chapter introduces a fictitious retail department store with four branch stores and one flagship store—with management and buying offices located at the flagship store—and the simulation associated with it. The customer profile, sales volume, and store design vary based on the characteristics of each location. In the simulation, you will play the role of a buyer and will follow a systematic plan to import jeans to Perry's distribution center located in Fredericksburg, Virginia, for one season.

It should be noted that a department store the size of Perry's would typically not be capable of importing products on its own due to the volume purchase requirement. Instead, the store would import through its buying office programs or by collaborating with a similar, but noncompetitive, store. However, for the purpose of the simulation, it is easier for you to complete the process as if Perry's were the sole importer.

OBJECTIVES OF THE SIMULATION

After completing the simulation, you will be able to:

* Understand a buyer's tasks when purchasing and importing product
* Discuss the dynamics of the international fashion marketplace
* Develop strategies for importing product

* Recognize and appreciate the culture and customs of other countries when working across borders

* Understand importing terms, policies, and laws

* Explore resources available to assist in importing

* Identify global resources to import product

* Complete the necessary forms to import product

THE SIMULATION: WHAT IS IT AND HOW DOES IT WORK?

A simulation can be defined as a situation that resembles something that exists in reality. For the sake of the simulation in this text, you will be provided with the statistical and demographic information necessary to make import-buying decisions. It will be your responsibility apply your logic and conduct additional research to substantiate your decisions to import product for the department store.

Perry's is fictitious, as is the statistical information provided, and is in no way representative of a specific retail organization.

PERRY'S DEMOGRAPHIC INFORMATION

Perry's is a small, suburban department store located in Fredericksburg, Virginia. The flagship store is located in the downtown area, with four branch operations located in surrounding shopping malls within a 40-mile radius of downtown.

Fredericksburg is located about 45 miles south of Washington, D.C., and about 45 miles north of Richmond, Virginia. Many residents in Fredericksburg and surrounding counties commute to work each day traveling north to Washington, D.C., by train to Union Station. For this reason, the area is considered a suburb of Washington, D.C., offering lower housing costs and living expenses. Other commuters travel south to Richmond, Virginia, either by car or by train. Fredericksburg and the surrounding counties of Stafford, Spotsylvania, and Caroline are rich in colonial, Revolutionary War, and Civil War history, each offering historic tourist attractions and plantations. There are four major Civil War battlefields in the area. The Fredericksburg and Spotsylvania Civil War National Military Park is the largest military monument in the United States with more than 5,500 acres. Three branches of the military, the Marines, navy, and army, have bases in the counties around Fredericksburg.

There is a walking tour of the 40 blocks in the Fredericksburg historic district where visitors can view many 18th- and 19th-century buildings. There are more than one hundred stores in which to shop, including four blocks of antiques. The Potomac and Rappahannock Rivers are close by for people interested in water activities. Several major companies employ many Fredericksburg-area residents. Both Capital One and Geico Direct have corporate offices in Fredericksburg, and the CVS drug chain operates a distribution center in the area. The city is also the home of Mary Washington College, a four-year liberal arts institution. Fredericksburg is a little more than ten square miles, with a population of about 20,000 and a median income of $34,585.

Stafford is primarily a rural county of 270 square miles situated 27 miles south of Washington, D.C. Quantico Marine base is located there as well as Ferry Farm estate, the childhood home of George Washington. The population is 111,021 and the median income is $66,809.

Spotsylvania County is south of Fredericksburg, just off I-95, 20 miles from Richmond. Lake Anna is one of the popular attractions in the area. The county covers 400 square miles, with an estimated population of 107,838 and a median income of $57,525.

Caroline County spans 533 square miles and is 30 miles north of Richmond. It is near Fort A. P. Hill, an army base. The county is mainly rural with a population of more than 23,000 and a median income of $39,845.

Dale City is located in Prince William County just 25 miles from Washington, D.C. The 15-square-mile city has a population of approximately 56,000 and a median income of $65,355. It is close to George Mason University in Fairfax, Marymount University in Arlington, Mary Washington College in Fredericksburg, and George Washington University and American University in Washington, D.C.

For more information on the Fredericksburg sector, a few suggested Web sites are www.simplyfredericksburg.com, www.fredericksburgvirginia.net, www.co.caroline.va.us, and www.census.gov. See Tables 01.01 through 01.05 for a demographic profile of each city or county.

TABLE 01.01

DEMOGRAPHIC PROFILE OF FREDERICKSBURG CITY, VA

CHARACTERISTICS	NUMBER	PERCENT	U.S.
GENERAL			
Total population	19,279	100.0	100%
Male	8,677	45.0	49.1%
Female	10,602	55.0	50.9%
Median age (years)	30.3	(X)	35.3
Under 5 years	1,127	5.8	6.8%
18 years and over	15,851	82.2	74.3%
65 years and over	2,470	12.8	12.4%
One race	18,904	98.1	97.6%
White	14,108	73.2	75.1%
Black or African American	3,935	20.4	12.3%
American Indian and Alaska Native	65	0.3	0.9%
Asian	291	1.5	3.6%
Native Hawaiian and Other Pacific Islander	11	0.1	0.1%
Some other race	494	2.6	5.5%
Two or more races	375	1.9	2.4%
Hispanic or Latino (of any race)	945	4.9	12.5%
Household population	16,960	88.0	97.2%
Group quarters population	2,319	12.0	2.8%
Average household size	2.09	(X)	2.59
Average family size	2.81	(X)	3.14
Total housing units	8,888	100.0	100.0%
Occupied housing units	8,102	91.2	91.0%
Owner-occupied housing units	2,882	35.6	66.2%
Renter-occupied housing units	5,220	64.4	33.8%
Vacant housing units	786	8.8	9.0%
SOCIAL			
Population 25 years and over	11,211	100.0	
High school graduate or higher	8,992	80.2	80.4%
Bachelor's degree or higher	3,423	30.5	24.4%
Civilian veterans (civilian population 18 years and over)	1,792	11.4	12.7%
Disability status (population 21 to 64 years)	2,345	21.9	19.2%
Foreign born	997	5.2	11.1%
Male, now married (population 15 years and over)	3,021	41.8	56.7%
Female, now married (population 15 years and over)	3,172	34.9	52.1%
Speak a language other than English at home (population 5 years and over)	1,746	9.6	17.9%
ECONOMIC			
In labor force (population 16 years and over)	10,906	67.5	63.9%
Mean travel time to work in minutes (population 16 years and over)	24.6	(X)	25.5
Median household income (dollars)	34,585	(X)	41,994
Median family income (dollars)	47,148	(X)	50,046
Per capita income (dollars)	21,527	(X)	21,587
Families below poverty level	408	10.4	9.2%
Individuals below poverty level	2,632	15.5	12.4%
HOUSING			
Single-family owner-occupied homes	2,712	100.0	
Median value (dollars)	135,800	(X)	119,600
With a mortgage	1,128	(X)	1,088
Not mortgaged	332	(X)	295

(X) Not applicable

SOURCE: U.S. Census Bureau (census 2000)

TABLE 01.02

DEMOGRAPHIC PROFILE OF STAFFORD COUNTY, VA

CHARACTERISTICS	NUMBER	PERCENT	U.S.
GENERAL			
Total population	92,446	100.0	100%
Male	46,486	50.3	49.1%
Female	45,960	49.7	50.9%
Median age (years)	33.1	(X)	35.3
Under 5 years	7,172	7.8	6.8%
18 years and over	63,277	68.4	74.3%
65 years and over	5,474	5.9	12.4%
One race	90,163	97.5	97.6%
White	75,807	82.0	75.1%
Black or African American	11,211	12.1	12.3%
American Indian and Alaska Native	417	0.5	0.9%
Asian	1,512	1.6	3.6%
Native Hawaiian and Other Pacific Islander	93	0.1	0.1%
Some other race	1,123	1.2	5.5%
Two or more races	2,283	2.5	2.4%
Hispanic or Latino (of any race)	3,342	3.6	12.5%
Household population	90,952	98.4	97.2%
Group quarters population	1,494	1.6	2.8%
Average household size	3.01	(X)	2.59
Average family size	3.32	(X)	3.14
Total housing units	31,405	100.0	100.0%
Occupied housing units	30,187	96.1	91.0%
Owner-occupied housing units	24,322	80.6	66.2%
Renter-occupied housing units	5,865	19.4	33.8%
Vacant housing units	1,218	3.9	9.0%
SOCIAL			
Population 25 years and over	56,029	100.0	
High school graduate or higher	49,650	88.6	80.4%
Bachelor's degree or higher	16,606	29.6	24.4%
Civilian veterans (civilian population 18 years and over)	12,713	21.2	12.7%
Disability status (population 21 to 64 years)	6,322	12.4	19.2%
Foreign born	3,713	4.0	11.1%
Male, now married (population 15 years and over)	21,618	63.6	56.7%
Female, now married (population 15 years and over)	21,824	64.2	52.1%
Speak a language other than English at home (population 5 years and over)	6,221	7.3	17.9%
ECONOMIC			
In labor force (population 16 years and over)	50,424	76.0	63.9%
Mean travel time to work in minutes (population 16 years and over)	37.7	(X)	25.5
Median household income (dollars)	66,809	(X)	41,994
Median family income (dollars)	71,575	(X)	50,046
Per capita income (dollars)	24,762	(X)	21,587
Families below poverty level	582	2.4	9.2%
Individuals below poverty level	3,138	3.5	12.4%
HOUSING			
Single-family owner-occupied homes	21,792	100.0	
Median value (dollars)	156,400	(X)	119,600
With a mortgage	1,363	(X)	1,088
Not mortgaged	313	(X)	295

(X) Not applicable   SOURCE: U.S. Census Bureau (census 2000)

TABLE 01.03

DEMOGRAPHIC PROFILE OF SPOTSYLVANIA COUNTY, VA

CHARACTERISTICS	NUMBER	PERCENT	U.S.
GENERAL			
Total population	90,395	100.0	100%
Male	44,532	49.3	49.1%
Female	45,863	50.7	50.9%
Median age (years)	34.3	(X)	35.3
Under 5 years	6,879	7.6	6.8%
18 years and over	63,287	70.0	74.3%
65 years and over	7,526	8.3	12.4%
One race	88,696	98.1	97.6%
White	74,924	82.9	75.1%
Black or African American	11,255	12.5	12.3%
American Indian and Alaska Native	288	0.3	0.9%
Asian	1,243	1.4	3.6%
Native Hawaiian and Other Pacific Islander	45	0.0	0.1%
Some other race	941	1.0	5.5%
Two or more races	1,699	1.9	2.4%
Hispanic or Latino (of any race)	2,536	2.8	12.5%
Household population	89,841	99.4	97.2%
Group quarters population	554	0.6	2.8%
Average household size	2.87	(X)	2.59
Average family size	3.22	(X)	3.14
Total housing units	33,329	100.0	100.0%
Occupied housing units	31,308	93.9	91.0%
Owner-occupied housing units	25,735	82.2	66.2%
Renter-occupied housing units	5,573	17.8	33.8%
Vacant housing units	2,021	6.1	9.0%
SOCIAL			
Population 25 years and over	56,633	100.0	
High school graduate or higher	47,446	83.8	80.4%
Bachelor's degree or higher	12,928	22.8	24.4%
Civilian veterans (civilian population 18 years and over)	10,910	17.4	12.7%
Disability status (population 21 to 64 years)	8,632	16.5	19.2%
Foreign born	2,917	3.2	11.1%
Male, now married (population 15 years and over)	21,459	65.7	56.7%
Female, now married (population 15 years and over)	21,777	62.2	52.1%
Speak a language other than English at home			
(population 5 years and over)	4,611	5.5	17.9%
ECONOMIC			
In labor force (population 16 years and over)	47,747	72.2	63.9%
Mean travel time to work in minutes (population 16 years and over)	37.1	(X)	25.5
Median household income (dollars)	57,525	(X)	41,994
Median family income (dollars)	62,422	(X)	50,046
Per capita income (dollars)	22,536	(X)	21,587
Families below poverty level	842	3.4	9.2%
Individuals below poverty level	4,247	4.7	12.4%
HOUSING			
Single-family owner-occupied homes	22,130	100.0	
Median value (dollars)	128,500	(X)	119,600
With a mortgage	1,147	(X)	1,088
Not mortgaged	282	(X)	295

(X) Not applicable   **SOURCE:** U.S. Census Bureau (census 2000)

TABLE 01.04

DEMOGRAPHIC PROFILE OF CAROLINE COUNTY, VA

CHARACTERISTICS	NUMBER	PERCENT	U.S.
GENERAL			
Total population	22,121	100.0	100%
Male	11,011	49.8	49.1%
Female	11,110	50.2	50.9%
Median age (years)	37.7	(X)	35.3
Under 5 years	1,381	6.2	6.8%
18 years and over	16,645	75.2	74.3%
65 years and over	2,857	12.9	12.4%
One race	21,819	98.6	97.6%
White	13,842	62.6	75.1%
Black or African American	7,604	34.4	12.3%
American Indian and Alaska Native	172	0.8	0.9%
Asian	79	0.4	3.6%
Native Hawaiian and Other Pacific Islander	6	0.0	0.1%
Some other race	116	0.5	5.5%
Two or more races	302	1.4	2.4%
Hispanic or Latino (of any race)	295	1.3	12.5%
Household population	21,543	97.4	97.2%
Group quarters population	578	2.6	2.8%
Average household size	2.69	(X)	2.59
Average family size	3.08	(X)	3.14
Total housing units	8,889	100.0	100.0%
Occupied housing units	8,021	90.2	91.0%
Owner-occupied housing units	6,571	81.9	66.2%
Renter-occupied housing units	1,450	18.1	33.8%
Vacant housing units	868	9.8	9.0%
SOCIAL			
Population 25 years and over	15,082	100.0	
High school graduate or higher	10,761	71.3	80.4%
Bachelor's degree or higher	1,821	12.1	24.4%
Civilian veterans (civilian population 18 years and over)	2,424	14.6	12.7%
Disability status (population 21 to 64 years)	2,692	21.4	19.2%
Foreign born	382	1.7	11.1%
Male, now married (population 15 years and over)	4,992	57.1	56.7%
Female, now married (population 15 years and over)	5,014	56.7	52.1%
Speak a language other than English at home (population 5 years and over)	556	2.7	17.9%
ECONOMIC			
In labor force (population 16 years and over)	11,025	63.9	63.9%
Mean travel time to work in minutes (population 16 years and over)	37.7	(X)	25.5
Median household income (dollars)	39,845	(X)	41,994
Median family income (dollars)	43,533	(X)	50,046
Per capita income (dollars)	18,342	(X)	21,587
Families below poverty level	438	7.2	9.2%
Individuals below poverty level	2,008	9.4	12.4%
HOUSING			
Single-family owner-occupied homes	4,735	100.0	
Median value (dollars)	88,900	(X)	119,600
With a mortgage	875	(X)	1,088
Not mortgaged	241	(X)	295

(X) Not applicable   **SOURCE:** U.S. Census Bureau (census 2000)

TABLE 01.05 Dalecity

DEMOGRAPHIC PROFILE OF ~~CAROLINE COUNTY~~, VA

CHARACTERISTICS	NUMBER	PERCENT	U.S.
GENERAL			
Total population	55,971	100.0	100%
Male	27,662	49.4	49.1%
Female	28,309	50.6	50.9%
Median age (years)	31.4	(X)	35.3
Under 5 years	4,496	8.0	6.8%
18 years and over	37,667	67.3	74.3%
65 years and over	2,108	3.8	12.4%
One race	53,491	95.6	97.6%
White	31,818	56.8	75.1%
Black or African American	16,099	28.8	12.3%
American Indian and Alaska Native	235	0.4	0.9%
Asian	2,840	5.1	3.6%
Native Hawaiian and Other Pacific Islander	107	0.2	0.1%
Some other race	2,392	4.3	5.5%
Two or more races	2,480	4.4	2.4%
Hispanic or Latino (of any race)	5,534	9.9	12.5%
Household population	55,930	99.9	97.2%
Group quarters population	41	0.1	2.8%
Average household size	3.17	(X)	2.59
Average family size	3.48	(X)	3.14
Total housing units	18,171	100.0	100.0%
Occupied housing units	17,623	97.0	91.0%
Owner-occupied housing units	13,712	77.8	66.2%
Renter-occupied housing units	3,911	22.2	33.8%
Vacant housing units	548	3.0	9.0%
SOCIAL			
Population 25 years and over	33,001	100.0	
High school graduate or higher	29,386	89.0	80.4%
Bachelor's degree or higher	7,485	22.7	24.4%
Civilian veterans (civilian population 18 years and over)	7,561	20.7	12.7%
Disability status (population 21 to 64 years)	4,652	14.4	19.2%
Foreign born	7,298	13.0	11.1%
Male, now married (population 15 years and over)	12,158	60.6	56.7%
Female, now married (population 15 years and over)	12,348	60.1	52.1%
Speak a language other than English at home (population 5 years and over)	9,505	18.4	17.9%
ECONOMIC			
In labor force (population 16 years and over)	30,704	77.6	63.9%
Mean travel time to work in minutes (population 16 years and over)	39.3	(X)	25.5
Median household income (dollars)	65,355	(X)	41,994
Median family income (dollars)	69,278	(X)	50,046
Per capita income (dollars)	22,363	(X)	21,587
Families below poverty level	442	3.1	9.2%
Individuals below poverty level	2,452	4.4	12.4%
HOUSING			
Single-family owner-occupied homes	13,139	100.0	
Median value (dollars)	134,100	(X)	119,600
With a mortgage	1,287	(X)	1,088
Not mortgaged	353	(X)	295

(X) Not applicable

SOURCE: U.S. Census Bureau (census 2000)

PERRY'S STATISTICAL INFORMATION

Perry's classifies its branch stores by a ranking of A, B, or C, according to sales volume and the progressive styling of the consumers who patronize each branch. Many department stores rank their branch stores using this alphabetical ranking system of A, B, C, D, E, and so on. Others may use similar methods. Some of the reasons stores are ranked in this manner are to plan or predict:

1. Square footage

2. Interior décor

3. Fixtures

4. Sales volume

5. Inventory levels

6. Stock assortment

7. Store personnel

8. Consumer profile

"A" stores have the highest sales volume and usually receive an additional layer of upscale fashion merchandise. Typically, "A" stores have a higher average purchase than "B" or "C" stores.

"B" stores have the second highest sales volume and inventory level. "C" stores are average, with a lower sales volume than "A" and "B" stores and an inventory that reflects the moderate taste level of an average consumer, the largest portion of the population.

At Perry's, A stores generate a sales volume close to or higher than $13 million and cater to a middle- to upper-income consumer with progressive to classic taste, one who probably commutes north to the metropolitan D.C. area. These consumers are white-collar professionals who work in office environments. Both the downtown Fredericksburg and Spotsylvania branch stores are A stores.

Perry's B stores produce a sales volume of between $9 and $10 million, from conservative, middle-income families who likely work within a 15- to 20-mile radius of the B stores. Style and value are equally important. The two B stores are in Stafford and Dale City.

Perry's has one C branch store with a sales volume of less than $5 million. Most of the customers shopping in this branch store consider value to be more important than

TABLE 01.06

TOTAL YEARLY SALES BY STORE

STORE CLASSIFICATION	LOCATION	SALES VOLUME	PERCENT OF TOTAL
A Store	Downtown	$13,650,000	27.3
A Store	Spotsylvania	13,200,000	26.4
B Store	Dale City	9,550,000	19.1
B Store	Stafford	9,100,000	18.2
C Store	Caroline	4,500,000	9.0
TOTAL		$50,000,000	100.0

style. A C-store consumer is generally a local or longtime resident of the area and probably lives in a rural region. The Caroline County store is a C store.

Table 01.06 shows how Perry's ranks its flagship and branch stores according to the sales volume and to the fashion demands of the consumers who frequent each branch.

PERRY'S: A TRADITIONAL ORGANIZATION

Perry's organization is a traditional department store, with five functions. The merchandise function involves purchasing merchandise, both domestic and import, for retail sale. The vice president of merchandise oversees general merchandise managers (GMMs), divisional merchandise managers (DMMs), buyers, and assistant buyers. The vice president of operations is responsible for handling all aspects of the retail stores. Warehouse and store managers, department sales managers, and salespeople report to the vice president of operations. The vice president of sales promotion is in charge of advertising, public relations, and visual merchandising. Accounts payable/receivable, inventory control, customer charge accounts, merchandise information systems, and finance departments are controlled by the vice president of finance. The vice president of human resources is responsible for hiring, training, and maintaining store personnel. Buyers at Perry's, as at any department store, must interact with all functions to maximize their department's potential and profit.

Buying and selling functions are separate at Perry's. This means that buyers do not directly supervise the sales staff. However, because of the proximity of the stores, buyers are significantly involved with sales training and merchandise layout for the departmental sales floor.

The responsibilities of a buyer employed by Perry's to buy domestic and imported merchandise include:

1. Developing a six-month dollar buying plan for domestic and imported goods for all five stores

2. Developing model stock plans by classification, subclassification, price line, color units, size, and fabrication for all five stores

3. Developing merchandise for import

4. Analyzing trends using the buying office as the main source

5. Analyzing vendor performance, including sales results and markdown dollars and percentage

6. Educating sales personnel about:
   a. Merchandising of new trends
   b. Sales floor layout
   c. Sales promotion and special events

7. Supervising assistant buyers or other buying office staff

8. Developing long-term departmental goals

9. Selecting merchandise at the domestic and overseas markets, according to approved plans

10. Accurately recording all purchases, transfers, and returns to vendors, which affect the value of departmental inventory

11. Planning sales promotions for the department, including advertising and special sales

12. Communicating with department sales managers

13. Communicating with the divisional merchandise manager and general merchandise manager

Buyers at Perry's purchase merchandise from domestic manufacturers as well as directly from overseas vendors. Buyers shop for the majority of merchandise from domestic manufacturers' in-line collections. They also work with manufacturers to custom develop product that will be either exclusively for their store or done as a joint venture with noncompeting stores. Working together with noncompeting stores generates a higher volume purchase, often needed to meet the ***minimum order quantity (MOQ)*** required by the manufacturer. Some domestic manufacturers give buyers the option of purchasing product through direct import (DI), or they deliver it to a ***port of entry (POE)*** close to the store distribution center. Many buyers travel overseas to visit factories and attend trade shows, buying merchandise directly from a factory, through direct import or POE. Buyers may also develop custom product to their specifications. The advantage of buying through direct import or POE is that the landed cost of the product is lower than the manufacturer's wholesale price; however, the quantity to fill a container may be more than what a buyer needs. Buyers will often place orders with more than one resource, consolidating orders from all factories to fill a container. In this case, the various resources deliver the ***less-than-container load (LCL)*** of purchased goods to the shipping company. The shipping company combines the merchandise to fill a container and ships the container to the store.

Competition
The largest mall in the Fredericksburg area is the Spotsylvania Mall, with four anchor department stores that compete with Perry's: Sears, JCPenney, Belk, and Hecht's. Kohl's department store has locations in both Fredericksburg and Stafford. Nordstrom stores are located north and south of Fredericksburg, while Dillard's stores aren't located further north than the Richmond area. The Potomac Mills Outlet shopping center is near the Fredericksburg area, boasting more than one hundred stores, such as Abercrombie & Fitch, American Eagle, Burlington Coat Factory, Gap, H&M, Hollister, JCPenney, L.L.Bean, Limited Too, Nautica, Nordstrom, Oshkosh, Polo Ralph Lauren, and Tommy Hilfiger, all featuring reduced prices. Because of the great offering of discount merchandise, Perry's buyers are very conscious of value pricing.

Merchandise Categories
Perry's Department Store carries men's, women's, and children's apparel and accessories, which the industry refers to as soft goods or soft lines. There is also a home store with gift and decorative accessories, domestics, tabletop, and housewares, often referred to as hard goods or hard lines. The simulation will focus on the import purchase of denim jeans. Denim is offered in men's, young men's, women's plus sizes, misses', petites', juniors', boys', girls', toddlers', infants', and newborns' departments.

Select one of these apparel areas to complete the import process for the simulation. You will need to research the size range and trends for the specific area.

Industry Overview of Denim

Denim jeans were first introduced by Levi Strauss in 1873 as work pants for miners during the California Gold Rush. Strauss designed the basic five-pocket jean out of a sturdy blue cotton fabric he called denim, placing rivets on the pocket corners for durability. Farmers, cowboys, and some factory workers wore denim to work. As time went on, denim jeans became more widely accepted as casual dress for all, with the basic jean now considered a classic garment for men and women of all ages. As the popularity of jeans has grown, so has the constant flow of trendy jeans. Women's jeans come in all lengths from short shorts to cropped to tall. The shape of the leg varies from straight to tapered to flared and waistlines come in natural waist and very low rise. Men and women choose from slim fit to relaxed fit. What once only came in basic blue now includes sandblast, dark, faded, distressed, stonewash, and more.

There are more than one hundred brands of jeans available at all price points. The Faded Glory brand of denim at Wal-Mart sells for around $20, but for leading brands such as Lucky, Sean Jean, James, and Joe's, prices range from $76 to $173. Popular designer jeans labels are DKNY, Armani, Dolce & Gabbana, Calvin Klein, Tommy Hilfiger, and Ralph Lauren. At Bloomingdale's, some denim jeans sell for more than $200. Higher priced jeans from just under $100 and up are referred to as premium jeans. Many teenagers buy jeans from specialty stores. Old Navy's average retail prices range from $20 to $40. The Gap and American Eagle both have average retail prices from $ 29.99 for sale jeans to $58 for fashion denim. Price does not appear to be an issue for the fashion conscious seeking a specific look or label.

See Sidebars 01.01, 01.02, and 01.03 for additional demographics on jeans from Cotton Incorporated.

PERRY'S DEPARTMENT STORE DENIM PRODUCT DEVELOPMENT

The denim classification at Perry's consists of a few brand-name jeans such as Levis, Union Bay, Calvin Klein, and Ralph Lauren. Oshkosh is the dominant label for newborns, infants, toddlers, boys, and girls. Young men and juniors choose from two to three trendy fashion labels that may change depending on the current trends. Depending on the department, designer labels account for around 10 to 20 percent of the inventory in denim, with young men and junior departments on the higher side.

Jeanology

Women stay true to the reasons they love denim

The more times change, the more things stay the same, goes the old adage. And when it comes to denim—and more particularly, women's fondness for it—that statement couldn't be truer.

When the Cotton Incorporated Lifestyle Monitor, conducted a comparison of consumer habits and preferences over the last 10 years, women of various generations stayed consistent in the attributes that they seek from their jeans.

When asked by the Monitor what their major priorities were when purchasing denim, female respondents favored practicality slightly more than appearance. Baby Boomers, aged 40 to 58 today, and women from the Greatest Generation, aged 59 to 70 today, were nearly identical in their demands on denim. In 1995, 61% of Baby Boomers and Greatest Generation consumers cited being practical as their major concern when purchasing denim. In 2004, that 61% held steady.

Generation X consumers, however, today aged 26 to 39, were more partial to denim's flattering appearance. In 1995, 52% of Gen Xers cited being practical while 48% claimed looking good was more important. In 2004, women of this generation stayed true to form, at 53% and 47% for practicality and appearance, respectively.

"Everyone loves denim because it's the easiest thing to throw on, and it always looks good," states David Shelist, founder of the Denim Lounge, a boutique in Chicago. "And denim goes with everything."

"Denim is pretty much as practical a fabric as you can get today," considers Claire Dupuis, senior trend forecaster with Cotton Incorporated. "You are just as likely to see it in the mall with a pair of tennis shoes, as you are on the red carpet with diamonds. Women love denim for its overwhelming versatility; it's the ultimate practical garment."

That most likely explains why they own so much of it. Gen Xers, Baby Boomers and women of the Greatest Generation claimed that they owned 8.12, 6.89 and 5.14 pairs of jeans, respectively, up slightly from the previous decade at 7.43, 6.62 and 4.83.

"Denim is truly a 24/7 type of fabric," continues Dupuis. "Women own so many pairs that they could wear a new pair every day for a week with no repeats."

Shelist can definitely attest to that. "I was at an extremely fancy cocktail party this past weekend and there were women there in denim," he

MAJOR CONCERN WHEN PURCHASING DENIM

Generation	GENERATION X		BABY BOOMERS		GREATEST GENERATION	
	1995	2004	1995	2004	1995	2004
	16–29	26–39	30–48	40–58	49–66	59–70
Looking Good	48%	47%	39%	38%	39%	39%
Being Practical	52%	53%	61%	62%	61%	61%

relates. "And you know what? They fit right in among the silks and velvets."

That certainly speaks of a new practicality to denim from its humble origins as a true working garment. "The market has evolved so much," asserts Michael Ball, designer and founder of premium denim label Rock & Republic. "While denim delivers both, it's function before fashion for most women."

"Trends come and go, but what denim usually comes down to is the basic five-pocket styling," says Lars Klingenstedt, creative director of merchandising/design for Carbon Denim, a moderately priced denim collection aimed at young women. "At any age, women want jeans that look good and provide the right fit." Adds Shelist, "We encourage women to try on as many pairs as they can carry, so that they can find that perfect fit. It's not necessarily about the latest and greatest, but it is always about the fit."

Agrees Cotton Incorporated's Dupuis, "Women all have different things they look for, but for the most part, I think it's about the waist to hip ratio." That assessment leads her to another point. "I think, because the waist is such a sensitive area for women, we're seeing the continued popularity of the low-rise pant. It fits the hip and you don't have to worry about the waist."

And don't discount the stitching, washes, finishes, cuts, tints and other novelty touches that keep women on the hunt for another new pair of jeans, say fashion experts.

"I think because women love denim, they're looking for a pair of jeans with the great fit they crave," say Ball of Rock & Republic, "so they seek a range of colors and textures, twills or cross hatches, so that they don't look like they're wearing the same pair of jeans every day. Only their comfort is consistent." He adds, "There are a dizzying amount of finishes out there that all relate to a particular trend. Take your pick."

The very last thing women are likely to be looking at is the label inside the jean, maintain Ball and Klingenstedt, who design and sell jeans at significantly different price points.

"Women care about what looks good and fits well," Klingenstedt relates.

Drawing the same conclusion is Ball from Rock & Republic. "There's a premium market dedicated to delivering a premium value," he says, "but spending $150 doesn't make it a serious value; that comes from how they fit, look and feel."

So whatever style, fit, price or treatment it comes in, one thing's for certain—American women will always remain true blue to denim!

This story is one in a series of articles based on findings from Cotton Incorporated's Lifestyle Monitor *tracking research. Each story will focus on a specific topic as it relates to the American women's wear consumer and her attitudes and behavior regarding clothing, appearance, fashion, fiber selection and many other timely, relevant subjects.*

SOURCE: *Lifestyle Monitor*, Cotton Incorporated, January 6, 2005, www.cottoninc.com/lsmarticles. © 2005 Cotton Incorporated. All rights reserved.

Dads & Denim

A tradition passed from generation to generation

Despite all the desperate housewives' complaints about their husbands, today's dads are actually more involved in parenting than ever before.

With all this extra involvement, dads are throwing on apparel that works for them—and a top choice is denim. Jeans are great for fixing a bike chain, sitting in sandy bleachers while watching the kids play sports, or going out for ice cream.

Jeans are also what most of today's fathers grew up in. The Sixties turned denim jeans into a staple item. So, little boys who dug for worms in their "dungarees" are now hauling their own kids out of Little Tikes sandboxes while still wearing denim as adults. It's what they grew up in, and it's what they live in still.

"I wear khakis to work, but as soon as I get home, I change into my jeans," says Dave, 35, a New Jersey–based executive recruiter. "I have two girls, and they want to play as soon as they see me. Plus my wife always has a list of things she wants me to do—whether it's yard work, fixing something.... My jeans aren't going to get ruined no matter what I'm doing for these guys."

According to Cotton Incorporated's Lifestyle Monitor, a whopping 70.5% of men prefer denim jeans to casual slacks. And when presented with the statement, "Jeans are in my past, not my future," 91% of respondents disagreed.

While Gap is opening a chain of stores for women in the "mom" phase of their lives, it currently has no plans to do the equivalent for men. However, it does have a new a line that seems tailor-made for fathers—Stressfree Easy Fit denim.

"Stressfree is definitely a great option for a dad because it stands up to spills and stains," says Erica Archambault, Gap spokesperson. She explains, "Liquids bead up and roll off the fabric and stains can't take hold. It's also a great option for the guy on the go who's drinking coffee on the way to work—and no doubt spilling it on some occasions."

The dads who wear denim range from the young Gen X crowd to older Baby Boomers. At Uptown Jean Co., which is based in Santa Barbara, CA, and has four stores in the Golden State, purchasing preferences are apparent.

"The younger dads are going to be a little more fashion-conscious, and they don't mind spending a little extra," says Jason Martin, men's buyer. "The dads in the middle usually buy what they like at the cheapest price. And the older dads are more about quality, and getting something that's going to last."

PREFER TO WEAR

	'03	'04	CHANGE
Casual Slacks	28.5%	26.0%	-2.5
Denim Jeans	69.8%	70.5%	0.7

Although looking good in their denim is becoming increasingly important, the Monitor finds that, for nearly 66% of men, practicality is the major concern when purchasing denim.

"It's definitely about comfort and what fits them well," Martin says. "It's also about versatility, so they can dress it up and down."

Lucky Brand is the top selling denim at Uptown Jean Co. "It has a great range of fits, and a lot of options as far as the leg and seat. It's a real guys kind of jean. And it could be because the fly says 'Lucky,'" Martin adds with a laugh. Uptown's dads also appreciate Mavi for its stretch, he says, and, if they're into a high-fashion jean, Energie.

At Gap, while younger customers might be willing to sacrifice comfort for style, "Dads are definitely less flexible and really hunt for the perfect-fitting jeans," says Archambault. Among the father favorites: Gap's boot-cut and loose, straight-fit jeans are two top sellers; easy and relaxed fit are also popular.

Levi's has been outfitting dads since they were young boys on the sandlot, keeping up with them as they've headed into fatherhood. And, over the years, the company has seen a difference in the way dads approach their denim.

"Dads are more fashion aware than ever before," affirms Amy Gemellaro, Levi spokesperson. "He has jeans by occasion now: his Saturday yard work jeans, casual Friday with a blazer jean, Saturday night date jean."

The Monitor finds that men own eight pairs of jeans, and wear five of them on a regular basis.

"Many men wear a low-waisted jean as a more sophisticated look, like our Levi's Premium 'The Skinner'; and a classic fit like the 501 or 505 for more conservative occasions. The 505 is a classic straight fit that's also very popular."

At Haggar, whose name is synonymous with wrinkle-resistant trousers, Comfort Equipped jeans were introduced two years ago after the success of its casual pants line bearing the same name. These bottoms are not a five-pocket jean; rather they're similar to a pair of khaki pants, explains Gary Aronson, senior vice president of merchandising.

The pant features a hidden expandable waistband, which allows for up to two inches of give, a welcome feature for many a dad—especially after a day-long barbecue. Aronson says he sees a difference between the Gen X dads versus the Boomer fathers.

"Over-40 men typically want comfort," he notes, explaining the success of the Comfort Equipped denim. However, Aronson adds, "The younger dads are still looking for the traditional five-pocket jean." To that end, Haggar is introducing a five-pocket Comfort Equipped jeans model scheduled for retail delivery in Spring 2006.

From Boomer to Gen X through Gen Y, there's no doubt that the dads and denim tradition is one that's bound to be passed down for many generations to come.

This story is one in a series of articles based on findings from Cotton Incorporated's Lifestyle Monitor *tracking research. Each story will focus on a specific topic as it relates to the American men's wear consumer and his attitudes and behavior regarding clothing, appearance, fashion, fiber selection and many other timely, relevant subjects.*

SOURCE: *Lifestyle Monitor*, Cotton Incorporated, May 30, 2005, www.cottoninc.com/lsmarticles. © 2005 Cotton Incorporated. All rights reserved.

Denim Jeans Command Loyalty

In an era of cross-shopping, brand proliferation, and declining prices, retailers and manufacturers are continuously looking to identify their true competition—usually by brand—and to develop strategies to combat apparel price deflation. In the 2003 winter edition of the Textile Consumer, "Measuring the Brand Premium," analysis of consumer purchase data indicated that very few consumers were loyal to specific brands or to a type of brand (national brands versus private labels). However, additional analysis has demonstrated that consumers are less likely to switch brand type when buying denim jeans than when buying other apparel products—implying that jeans command more brand loyalty. The analysis presented here can help retailers and manufacturers to better understand the denim jeans market and to develop tactical marketing techniques.

Measuring Customer Loyalty to Brand Types
Consumers are loyal to denim jeans brand types: over the past three years, more than 8 of 10 of denim jeans customers purchased exclusively either national brands or private labels, based on survey data from STS Market Research. Overall, more consumers bought national-brand than private-label denim jeans (72% vs. 47%), consistent with the fact that national-brand jeans outsold private-label jeans (60% to 40% in 2003 on a unit basis). Of consumers who bought denim jeans, 53% bought only national brands, 28% bought only private labels, and 19% bought both (i.e., cross-shopped between brand types). To assess brand-type loyalty, it is useful to consider separately those consumers who bought at least one pair of national-brand jeans (72% of the consumers sampled) and those who bought at least one pair of private-label jeans (47% of the consumers). Their "loyalty" can be measured as the percentage who bought only that brand type (i.e., did not cross-shop). Among consumers who purchased any national-brand jeans, 74% bought only national brands, while 26% also bought private labels. Among consumers who purchased any private-label jeans, 59% bought only private labels, while 41% bought national brands as well. These figures support the idea that consumers tend to be loyal to brand types, and especially to national brands. Loyalty to national brands was

CONSUMERS CROSS-SHOPPING BETWEEN BRAND TYPES

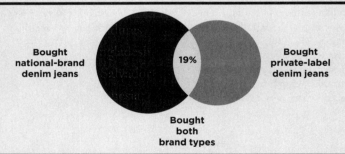

Bought national-brand denim jeans

19%

Bought private-label denim jeans

Bought both brand types

SOURCE: Based on data from STS Market Research

% OF CONSUMERS WHO PURCHASED APPAREL ONLY WITHIN ONE BRAND TYPE

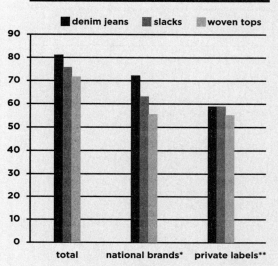

SOURCE: Based on data from STS Market Research

The Roots of Brand-Type Loyalty

Brand-type loyalty may be influenced by such attributes as quality, style, and labeling. Other possible explanations for loyalty to national-brand denim jeans are their greater availability and a greater opportunity to buy national brands at sale prices. National-brand merchandise is more accessible because it is available at numerous retailers, while private-label merchandise is available only at select stores. Furthermore, although private-label jeans sell for less than national brands on average ($22.71 vs. $23.04), they are less likely to be sold at marked-down prices. In 2003, 48% of national-brand jeans were sold at a discount, compared with 32% of private-label jeans. Slashing of prices creates a perceived value to consumers and attracts bargain hunters, even if they still pay more than for competing products.

Men's Greater Loyalty

Loyalty to denim jeans brand types differs significantly by gender. Since 2001, 22% of women purchased both private-label and national-brand denim jeans, compared with 18% of men. Of consumers who purchased national-brand jeans, 79% of men and 68% of women bought only national brands, and among consumers who purchased private-label jeans, 60% of men and 56% of women bought only private labels. Research from Cotton Incorporated's Lifestyle Monitor offers a possible explanation for men's greater loyalty to brand type: only 22% of men like or love to shop for clothing, compared with 57% of women. Men also are willing to pay a slightly higher price for jeans than women are ($24.26, compared with $23.15). Buying the same brand time after time, even if it

significantly higher for denim jeans than for other apparel products, such as slacks or woven tops. Among consumers who purchased slacks, 76% bought only one brand type, and among purchasers of woven tops, 72% were loyal to a single brand type. As shown in the graph above, loyalty among consumers who purchased national brands was markedly lower for slacks (63%) and woven tops (56%) than for jeans (74%). In contrast, loyalty to private labels was similar among purchasers of jeans (59%), slacks (58%), and woven tops (56%).

means paying a bit more, tends to expedite the shopping experience. Thus, men's greater brand loyalty may be due in part to their desire to get in and out of the store as quickly as possible.

Loyalty and Age
Age is another determinant of brand-type loyalty. Young people (under 35) were generally more likely than their elders to cross-shop between brand types. However, patterns of cross-shopping with age differed between male and female consumers. Cross-shopping was highest (25%) among women aged 19 to 24 and dropped off sharply among women over 34. Women's loyalty to both national brands and private labels increased with age, though loyalty to national brands was consistently stronger. Among women who purchased any national-brand jeans, 75% of those aged 45 or older bought only national brands, compared with 67% of those under 45. Among women who purchased any private-label jeans, the corresponding figures were 63% for older women and 59% for younger women. These buying patterns probably reflect women's declining interest in fashion experimentation with age. Among male consumers, the cross-shopping picture was more complex. Overall, cross-shopping peaked among men aged 25 to 44 (at 22%) and was lowest among those over 54 (12%). Male consumers under 25 cross-shopped less than the 25- to 44-year-olds, but more than men over 44. This pattern seems to result from differences with age in men's loyalty to the two brand types. Among men who bought national-brand jeans, loyalty

CROSS-PURCHASERS OF DENIM JEANS
BRAND TYPES BY AGE AND GENDER
(2001–03)

% of consumers purchasing both national brands & private labels			
AGE GROUP	TOTAL	WOMEN	MEN
13–18	20.3	21.5	18.5
19–24	21.3	24.9	16.2
25–34	21.4	20.5	21.9
35–44	18.1	14.5	22.0
45–54	14.5	11.3	17.5
55–64	15.1	17.7	12.3
65+	13.5	14.7	12.2
All	19.0	21.5	18.5

SOURCE: Based on data from STS Market Research

generally increased with age (from 72% among male teens to 86% among men over 44). But among men who bought private-label jeans, loyalty was highest among the youngest and oldest consumers (over 60% for those under 25 or over 64) and was lowest by far (44%) in the 25 to 34 age group. Nearly a third of all male consumers under 25 purchased only private-label jeans, but the figure dropped dramatically (to 16%) among 25- to 34-year-olds, while the percentage wearing only national-brand jeans jumped to 57%. The greatest brand-type loyalty seen in any age and gender group was that of men aged 45 to 54 who bought national-brand jeans—only 13.5% of these consumers also bought private-label jeans.

SOURCE: *Textile Consumer*, Cotton Incorporated, Summer 2004, pp. 1–3. © 2004 Cotton Incorporated. All rights reserved.

Approximately 25 percent of the stock for all departments, except those for newborns, infants, and toddlers, is private label, developed by the buyer in conjunction with the buying office. The remainder is made up of well-known moderately priced denim resources. Newborn, infant, and toddler departments mostly carry popular brands, as there is not enough volume to warrant the purchase of private-label jeans. Perry's does not carry premium jeans.

There are several methods of selection for private-label jeans. When working on import purchases through the buying office, buyers submit their best-selling jeans for review to be knocked off. A knockoff is a copy of a style that has minor differences from the original, without sacrificing the qualities that resulted in the item becoming a best-seller. Buyers can also work directly with a designer to create a style. The designer may work for the buying office, factory, or vendor producing the garment. It is wise to base a volume purchase on a proven style to maximize sales. If an imported design does not sell well, the buyer will be stuck with a high dollar markdown to get rid of the large number of jeans.

Designers provide buyers with a working sketch, called a croquis, for approval. If creating a knockoff of a best-seller, and for an approved croquis, the next step is to create flats, or detailed drawings that include the garment's specifications. Most flats today are generated with a computer through a CAD (computer-aided design) program. While style is of utmost importance, price is the leading factor in the decision to import denim for Perry's. Careful consideration is crucial when determining details such as fabric content and weight, buttons, zippers, number of pockets, stitching, and embroidery. Finishing processes, packaging, labels, and hangtags also add to the garment's cost.

As a buyer for Perry's, you have been working with a factory overseas and have just completed product development of denim jeans for your department. The style of jeans has been finalized, size specifications confirmed, estimated landed cost and retail price established, and sample approved. The divisional merchandise manager has given approval to purchase a container of jeans for the upcoming season from overseas. The jeans will be an exclusive for Perry's at a competitive price to build margin for the department. Further details of the purchase will be discussed when the cost sheet is completed in Step Six.

The eight steps to develop your plan to import denim jeans are as follows:

STEP I   Profile the country selected to export denim

STEP II   Analyze the country selected for export feasibility

STEP III	Research business etiquette for the country of export
STEP IV	Examine import/export agreements
STEP V	Classify the product to be imported
STEP VI	Complete the cost sheet for the imported product
STEP VII	Determine the shipping route for the merchandise to be imported
STEP VIII	Finalize the entry process of the imported item

There are guidelines for each step of the plan. Remember to support your decisions and selections with research and facts.

CHAPTER 2

STEP ONE

Country Profile

Textiles and Apparel in the Global Marketplace

IN THIS CHAPTER, YOU WILL LEARN:

* The dynamics of the global textile and apparel industry
* The definitions of social, political, cultural, economical, and geographical traits of nations
* The importance of economic advancement among developed, developing (newly developed industrialized countries), and less-developed countries
* The state of the textile and apparel industries in major countries
* The role of international fashion centers

Retailers are developing their own product on a consistent basis to maintain lower costs and higher profit margins. More than 97 percent of all textiles and apparel product are produced outside of the United States. As a buyer for Perry's Department Store, you are working with a manufacturer off-shore to produce your jeans. You have compared the costs of domestic manufacturing and offshore manufacturing and have decided that it is more cost-effective to produce in another country. See Table 02.01 for the comparison of domestic versus offshore production.

Your first step in the simulation is to do research so you can prepare to work across borders. Remember that you are working with a country that has characteristics that are different from your own. The value system, communication levels, and time zones are examples of things you need to understand to function as an industry professional in a foreign country.

TABLE 02.01

COST TO MANUFACTURE A PAIR OF PANTS

	DOMESTIC PRODUCTION	OFFSHORE PRODUCTION
FABRIC	$5.90	$2.25
NOTIONS & TRIM Button Thread Zipper	1.19	.62
PACKING & TAGGING	.75	.40
LABOR Cutting Sewing Marking Grading	20.00	1.75
SHIPPING Freight	4.00	1.00
DUTY	0	3.00
COST	31.84	9.02

GLOBAL DYNAMICS OF THE TEXTILE AND APPAREL INDUSTRY

Almost every country in the world contributes to the textile and apparel marketplace. The textile and apparel industry employs more people worldwide than any other industry. As a result of *globalization*, and more recently regionalization, manufacturing has increasingly gone offshore for the purpose of reducing supply chain costs. As the con-

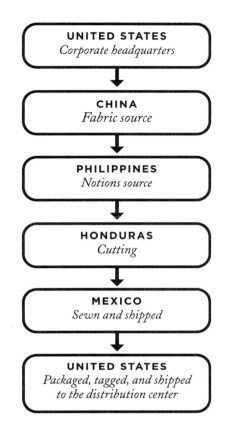

FIGURE 02.01: *Example of how a company can use multiple countries to manufacture one garment*

sumer demands quicker availability and trendier fashion, the fashion companies must bring product to market faster. The supply chain is the focus of manufacturers and retailers as they attempt to cut costs and time for textile and apparel production.

As many as five countries can contribute to manufacturing just one garment. Why would a company go to such trouble to move products in and out of countries, or to put it more formally, import and export from one country to another? The bottom line for most apparel and textile companies is cost of production and lead time. It is maybe cost-effective to have clothing cut in one country, sewn in another, packed in another, and shipped to the distribution center. See Figure 02.01.

TRAITS OF NATIONS

The traits of a nation can have a powerful impact on the way buyers conduct business. As a buyer you must be aware of the social, geographical, political, cultural, and economic traits of a nation.

Social Traits

Social traits refer to the language, education, values, and customs shared by the people of one country. In one culture, it may be acceptable to shake hands upon greeting people, while in another, a kiss on the cheek may be acceptable. A nation may view the role of women as insignificant and the role of men as superior and, therefore, only want to conduct business with male counterparts.

Geographical Traits

Geographical traits refer to the natural resources that are available in a country. It is important for buyers to note the ports, major waterways, and whether the country is landlocked.

Political Traits

Political traits usually relate directly to a nation's economy. The political environment of a nation can affect the flow of business daily. While many nations lean toward democratic types of government, those that are still autocratic are difficult to work with because decision making is usually done by the governing body without regard for the rights of individual businesses.

Cultural Traits

The **cultural traits** of a country have an impact on business etiquette. Culture is a mindset that is acquired and developed over time. It is a set of values shared by a group of people.

Economic Traits

Economic traits refer to the amount of goods and services that a nation produces and consumes, as well as the financial well-being of a country. A country's financial status can have an effect on the business conducted in it.

Globalization has helped many nations to gain momentum toward greater economic and technological independence characterized by denationalization. Denationalization refers to a country's boundaries becoming less important, thus, allowing more freedom in trade among nations.

Globalization has reshaped the fashion industry. It has shifted manufacturing from the United States to various countries around the world. This shift has caused an economic slowdown in some countries, but a major boost to an economy in other countries. Fashion companies have had to change the way they operate and become globalized: they conduct business in other countries whether it is manufacturing or seeking to enter a market for the purpose of selling their product.

As a result of producing in other countries, the fashion industry has played a role in helping countries to become industrialized. Examining developed, developing, and less-developed countries will provide a new understanding of the environment from which jeans are produced and imported.

Countries are usually defined by their gross domestic product (GDP), which is the amount of goods and services produced by a country in a one-year period. GDP does not include a nation's exports and imports, but rather the output of merchandise produced in the nation. GDP does not include the income that is generated from a nation's internationally owned companies. Alternatively, *gross national product* (GNP) is the value of all goods and services produced by a nation during a one-year period, and includes the income generated by domestic and internationally owned companies. Table 02.02 shows the top ten countries ranked by their GDP. This is an important economic indicator as it shows a nation's wealth.

Developed Countries

Developed countries have strong economies as a result of high levels of industrialization. They tend to conduct business abroad as well as at home. Their technology is advanced and the people have high standards of living. Developed countries have high levels of industrialization and very strong infrastructure. Infrastructure is defined as the state of resources and framework from which the industry and people work and operate within a country, including transportation, communication, and utility services.

Developing or Newly Industrialized Countries

Developing or newly industrialized countries are countries that are just beginning to become industrialized. They are in the process of moving from a less-developed status

TABLE 02.02

COUNTRIES WITH THE HIGHEST GDP

RANK	COUNTRY	GDP 2000 IN US$	GDP 2003 IN US$	CHANGE 2000/2003
1	United States	9,762,099,953,664	10,881,610,000,000	11.47%
2	Japan	4,763,832,811,520	4,326,444,000,000	-9.18%
3	Germany	1,870,276,460,544	2,400,655,000,000	28.36%
4	United Kingdom	1,437,994,713,088	1,794,858,000,000	24.82%
5	France	1,308,399,370,240	1,747,973,000,000	33.60%
6	Italy	1,074,762,612,736	1,465,895,000,000	36.39%
7	China	1,080,741,396,480	1,409,852,000,000	30.45%
8	Spain	561,376,854,016	836,100,300,000	48.94%
9	Canada	706,646,638,592	834,390,200,000	18.08%
10	South Asia	596,633,190,400	755,771,800,000	26.67%

SOURCE: www.geohive.com

to becoming more independent. The educational and technological resources are in a state of improvement and growth.

Less-Developed Countries

Less-developed countries have incomes that are at poverty level. The nation has limited natural resources, an unstable political situation, and extremely high unemployment rates. The people do not have adequate health care and shelter. Look at Table 02.03 and see if you can determine which countries are less-developed, newly developed, or developing.

THE STATE OF THE TEXTILE AND APPAREL INDUSTRIES IN SELECTED COUNTRIES

United States

U.S. apparel imports account for the majority of the U.S. apparel sold in 2003, with imports making up 96.6 percent of the U.S. market, the same as in 2002. Only 3.4 percent of textiles and apparel are produced in the United States. The high percentage of imports is mostly attributed to cheaper labor offshore, which lowers the cost of apparel to consumers. In 1997, there were 5,117 textile companies and 6,134 plants according

TABLE 02.03

WHICH COUNTRY IS DEVELOPED, DEVELOPING, OR LESS DEVELOPED?

	DEVELOPED	DEVELOPING	LESS DEVELOPED
Afghanistan			
Africa			
Australia	X		
Bangladesh			
Brazil		X	
Cambodia			X
China		X	
El Salvador			
Egypt		X	~~X~~
Japan	X		
Kenya			
Korea	X		
Mexico			
New Zealand	X		
Peru			
Philippines			
Rwanda			
Thailand			
Turkey		X	
United States	X		
Vietnam			

TABLE 02.04

TOP 25 COUNTRIES THAT IMPORT
TEXTILES AND APPAREL INTO THE UNITED STATES

	RANK	COUNTRY	% OF IMPORTS
		World	100
	1	China	27.8
	2	Mexico	7.8
	3	Honduras	5.5
✓	4	Bangladesh	5.0
	5	El Salvador	3.9
✓	6	Indonesia	3.7
✓	7	India	3.6
✓	8	Vietnam	3.6
	9	Dominican Republic	3.3
✓	10	Cambodia	3.1
✓	11	Pakistan	2.5
✓	12	Thailand	2.4
	13	Hong Kong	2.4
	14	Phillipines	2.3
	15	Guatemala	2.2
	16	Sri Lanka	2.1
	17	Taiwan	1.7
	18	South Korea	1.6
	19	Costa Rica	1.3
	20	Macau	1.2
	21	Jordan	1.2
	22	Turkey	1.1
	23	Malaysia	0.9
	24	Nicaragua	0.9
	25	Canada	0.9

SOURCE: Data from Apparel & Footwear Association. Reprinted courtesy of American Apparel & Footwear Association.

to the American Textile Manufacturers Institute. Overall, consumption of apparel rose 9.8 percent in 2003, reaching almost 16.5 billion garments.

The demand for textiles and apparel is far greater in the United States than it is in any other part of the world. As a result of the demand for fashion, a garment's life is short lived from its introduction to its decline; thus, the term *fast fashion* evolved. Fast fashion is based on the business strategy called Quick Response. **Quick Response**, as outlined by the Management Systems Committee of the American Apparel Manufacturers Association, is "a management philosophy since it embraces actions by the functions of a business, working in concert with each other. It also involves working in concert with suppliers and customers in meaningful, in-depth trading partners alliances using uniform, standard procedures. This alliance has mutual objectives of increased sales and profitability and reduced inventory for all partners." It is a combination of techniques that a business uses during all stages of production, from the procurement of raw materials, to the delivery of the finished product to the consumer. Keeping the cost of production down requires that manufacturing take place outside of the United States. The next part of the chapter examines the state of the fashion-producing industry around the world. Table 02.04 shows the top 25 countries in the world that import apparel into the United States. They account for almost 89 percent of the apparel imports.

East Asia

The countries of China, Japan, Hong Kong (special administrative region of China), South Korea, and Taiwan rank among the world's highest suppliers for exports of textiles and apparel. They accounted for one-fourth of the world's exports during the period from 1997 to 2001.

CHINA

It has been said that China is made for manufacturing. Production has grown from producing low- and medium-quality levels to producing designer ready-to-wear garments. Since 1976, when foreign trade was opened in China, its economy has continued to increase. China is the top producer of apparel based on quality of production, lead time, pricing, and quantity. It had 16 percent of the world's exports of textile and apparel in 2001. While China is a leader in apparel production, they must import most of their raw materials to produce textiles, except for silk.

JAPAN

Although fashion businesses dot the map of Japan, Tokyo is the principal site of production. Japan's role in the fashion industry includes working on both original design and manufacture of merchandise for foreign companies.

HONG KONG

Hong Kong has become an important player in the production of textiles and apparel. Possessing a highly competitive free-market economy, it is dependent upon international trade. The apparel sector is its largest manufacturing employer. In the early 1990s it became one of the world's leading clothing exporters and continues to hold its position today. As Hong Kong's economy strengthens so does the labor wage. Today, Hong Kong competes on service and outstanding workmanship rather than on low-wage labor. Major players in the fashion industry such as Nike, Liz Claiborne, and Esprit have manufacturing plants in Schezwan, China, while maintaining offices in Hong Kong.

TAIWAN AND SOUTH KOREA

The United States and Japan helped to develop Taiwan's textile industry. From about 1970 until 1995 it was considered one of the top three textile- and apparel-producing countries in the world. Today, the textile- and apparel-producing offices remain in Taiwan, but the production facilities are located in China. This is the trend between China and other East Asian suppliers to China. The average cost-per-operator hour, including social benefits, in spinning and weaving for 2002 was $0.69 in China compared with $6.15 in Hong Kong, $5.73 in South Korea, and $7.15 in Taiwan (Werner International Management consultants, Internet Assessment). The Taiwan Textile Federation is a supportive organization that represents all segments of the textile and apparel industry.

South Korea's industrialization can be attributed to the growth of textile and apparel production beginning in the early 1960s. The textile and apparel industry helped South Korea become a developing country. The biggest problem South Korea faces today is its inability to produce goods quickly. This is due to less technologically advanced factories and a shortage of labor. The industry is addressing both issues with South Korea as well as foreign investors.

FIGURE 02.02: *An international buyer and agent working with Cosmique Global at the Indian Handicraft and Gift Fair*

ASEAN

The Association of Southeast Asian Nations (ASEAN) includes Bangladesh, India, Pakistan, Vietnam, Cambodia, Indonesia, Laos, and Sri Lanka. Figure 02.02 shows international buyers working in a textile booth at the Indian Handicraft and Gift Fair. As with China, the countries in the ASEAN benefit from low wages. Vietnam and Cambodia are two of the world's fastest growing exporters of textiles and apparel in the world. The competition from the quotas lifted in 2005 under the Multi-Fiber Agreement governed under the World Trade Organization (WTO) has had an impact on competition.

Caribbean Countries

The major exporters in the Caribbean Basin are made up of Costa Rica, Dominican Republic, El Salvador, Guatemala, Haiti, Honduras, Jamaica, and Nicaragua. Since 1983, the CBI countries have increased their manufacturing production imports as a result of several things: Korea and Taiwan have made significant investments in these countries, the United States liberalized apparel quotas, and there is an expanded use of production-sharing operations in the region by U.S. apparel producers.

Andean Countries

Andean countries that produce textiles and apparel include Bolivia, Colombia, Ecuador, and Peru. Most imports came from Peru and Columbia, 49 percent and 46 percent, respectively, with cotton accounting for the vast majority of U.S. imports. Most of the increase in imports since 2000 has been a result of quotas being met in Asian countries.

Sub-Saharan Africa

Sub-Saharan Africa includes Kenya, Lesotho, Madagascar, Mauritius, and South Africa. The majority of production and exports from sub-Saharan Africa is apparel. The apparel industry is not as sophisticated in this part of the world as it is in other parts. Apparel production consists mostly of T-shirts, wovens, and some trousers. Foreign investors have not been as excited to put money into this part of the world because of political instability.

Egypt, Jordan, and Turkey

The third largest industry in Egypt is textiles and apparel. One-third of the employment in these countries comes from the manufacturing of textiles and apparel. Currently, Egypt's government still controls most of the country's manufacturing; however, in recent years it is starting to privatize the industry as a result of globalization. Egypt is a source of raw materials, especially cotton.

Most of Jordan's textile and apparel industry involves cut-sew-pack performances. The manufacturing is limited due to the scarce water supply, which is needed to operate the plants. Its textile and apparel sector has grown since 1996 when the United States provided legislation to establish "qualified industrial zones," which means goods can enter the United States duty free.

Textile and apparel manufacturing is the largest sector in Turkey. It is the seventh largest exporter of apparel and fourteenth largest textile exporter. The country's infrastructure is very modern. It is able to supply all facets of the supply chain process in one location with a skilled workforce.

Europe

France, England, and Italy have long attracted international attention for their high fashion. Paris, France, continues to attract some of the most creative and innovative designers in the world. One reason may be because the government of France is very supportive of the fashion industry.

London, England, is known for fine tailoring and ready-to-wear clothing. It has always been known for menswear, and Savile Row, which is where London's classic clothing can be found. Italy has long been known for quality fabrics and most notably leather. In the past five years Spain has emerged as a manufacturing center known to the rest of the world.

Germany is home to more than 2,000 manufacturers of textiles, apparel, and home fashions. Germany is a highly industrialized country with state-of-the-art manufacturing. Within the past two years, the German people have demanded more fashionable merchandise. Germany is slowly developing a reputation for innovative fashion.

The skilled labor force in Eastern Europe has grown extensively since the early 1990s, making the region an important production center for the world. Liz Claiborne, Macy's, Levi Strauss, and Vanity Fair are just a few companies that do business in the Eastern Bloc.

By 1993, Poland became one of Europe's largest CMT-clothing producers. The privatization of many Polish textile companies helped to restructure the Polish fashion industry in the early 1990s. Today, Poland has a high degree of import penetration, and the production industry seems to be slowing down.

The Czech Republic attracted many investors in the 1990s, mostly from Germany. In early 2000, there was a slow rise of production, which caused Czech textiles to outsource and add production plants.

Hungary's transition from a socialist economy to a market economy has helped it to compete internationally. There has also been a surge of foreign investments in the country's textile and apparel industry since the middle 1990s. Hungary is very fashion forward. As a result, it is starting to import more apparel to appease the demand for fashion items. Increasing salaries have enabled Hungarians to buy luxury clothing as well as inexpensive imports from China.

The Eastern Bloc nations of Latvia, Lithuania, and Estonia are up-and-coming textile and apparel production centers. These countries have been quite successful in attracting foreign investors. Latvia is a very small country but has a very high GDP growth rate compared with other countries in Europe. With a very strong and educated population, Lithuania boasts an annual production of 50 million pieces of knitwear; 40 million pairs of pantyhose, socks, and stockings; plus different types of fibers and fabrics. The major concern about its status as a production center is that it outsources production to nearby countries. Estonia is a very small country that is working very hard to develop its own production center and has been quite successful in attracting new customers. Its strength lies in the textile sector where it has doubled production from 8 percent in 1995 to 16 percent in 2002.

ROLE OF INTERNATIONAL FASHION CENTERS

As manufacturing has moved offshore, so have the fashion centers. The heart of the fashion industry is not confined to New York City or Paris. Fashion centers can be found throughout the world in places such as Tokyo, Japan, and Ho Chi Minh City, South Vietnam.

A fashion center usually consists of clusters of buildings that house showrooms representing manufacturers. The manufacturers can be recognizable brand names, such as Polo Ralph Lauren and Liz Claiborne, or they can just as easily be an unknown brand. Fashion centers are not limited to apparel. In New York City, the fashion center is clustered into apparel buildings, accessories and jewelry, trimming and manufacturing, and warehouse and offices.

Other fashion centers are located in Milan, Italy; London, England; Montreal, Quebec; Dusseldorf, Germany; Buenos Aires, Argentina; Sao Paulo, Brazil; Tokyo, Japan; China; and Hong Kong.

Most countries have their own textile and apparel associations, which sponsor fashion and market weeks throughout the year. These events attract buyers from all over the world. The fashion industry is truly operating in a global economy.

You are now ready to profile the country from which you will be importing jeans for Perry's Department Store. Using a minimum of five sources, profile the country from which you are going to import your jeans. The Central Intelligence Agency's *World Factbook,* which is on the Web at www.cia.gov/publications/factbook/, is an excellent resource. It contains a profile of every country in the world, which are updated regularly. You can find other resources in the "Country Profile Information" section of the Helpful Web Site Resources in the book and CD-ROM.

Create your own country profile by following the outline below. You should write out the information in an objective format, using an outline form. This should not be in essay form.

SIMULATION:
Go to the country profile worksheet on the CD-ROM and Helpful Web Site Resources in the book or CD-ROM.

COUNTRY
TRAITS OF THE COUNTRY
   Social
   Political
   Cultural
   Economic
   Geographic
CONTRIBUTING FACTORS
   Labor
   Inputs
   Products
   Transportation
   Business climate
EFFECTS OF QUOTA REMOVAL

CHAPTER 3

STEP TWO

Country Analysis

The Sourcing Decision: Strategies Used for Importing

IN THIS CHAPTER, YOU WILL LEARN:

* Why product is imported from foreign resources
* How to analyze a country to determine suitability for importing
* How to locate suppliers within a country to manufacture a specific product
* What factors should be considered prior to selecting a resource from a foreign country

Most companies decide to import from other countries to obtain products at lower prices or because a product is unique and not available in an existing market. There are many factors to consider when choosing a country from which to import raw material or in which to produce a commodity. The primary consideration is to determine what countries have the necessary raw materials or manufacture the type of products you wish to import. Once the eligible countries are determined, it is important to consider the foreign exchange rate for each country. How is the importer required to pay for the order? Does the importer need a letter of credit, or will a wire transfer be acceptable?

Investigate the stability of the countries. Is there social unrest, history of natural disasters, or other conditions that may delay or affect the manufacture of goods? If the government is unstable, or is at war with another country, it may be difficult for a country to export merchandise. During the summer in China, there are often blackouts due to power shortages. Without power, factories shut down, which delays production of goods.

After the importer chooses a country from which to import products, the next step is for the importer to locate a supplier within the country. The two most important concerns are the quality of the product and the reliability of the factory. It is helpful if the importer is able to contact other customers of the supplier for references. The importer should also visit the factory to inspect the facilities and observe the manufacturing process. If the quality of the product is poor, or the factory is unable to deliver merchandise in a timely manner, the result will be sales losses for the importer. Ask the factory the lead-time needed for production. It may be as few as 45 days or as much as 90 days or more. A credit report is also valuable as part of the evaluation of a potential source. Two means of obtaining credit reports are from Dun & Bradstreet or the U.S. Department of Commerce.

When visiting the factory, the importer should determine whether the company adheres to international laws. The Bureau of International Labor Affairs (ILAB) formulates and assists in supporting international labor policy as well as economic, immigration, and trade policies. One outstanding social issue is the use of child labor in factories. Some stores demand that factories sign a document stating they do not utilize child labor.

The textile and apparel industry continues to address ongoing problems associated with child labor and working conditions in foreign countries. The U.S. Department of Labor recognizes the problems of using child labor for the manufacturing process. The International Labor Organization (ILO) has estimated that 250 million children between the ages of 5 and 14 work in developing countries—at least 120 million of whom do so on a full-time basis. Sixty-one percent of these are in Asia, 32 percent in Africa, and 7 percent in Latin America. Most working children in rural areas work in agriculture; many children work as domestics; urban children work in trade and services, with fewer in manufacturing and construction (http://www.hrw.org/children/labor.htm).

In 1996, the U.S. Department of Labor collected information from 48 U.S. apparel importers and conducted site visits to 6 countries producing for the U.S. market. Upon analysis of the information collected, a report titled "The Apparel Industry and Codes of Conduct: A Solution to the International Child Labor Problem?" was written. The report states that codes of conduct vary from company to company with regard to standards for child labor and working conditions. Various codes of labor were found depending upon the company:

1. prohibitions on child labor

2. prohibitions on forced labor

3. prohibitions on discrimination based on race, religion, or ethnic origin

4. requirements to ensure the workers' health and safety of the workplace

COMPANY X SOURCING GUIDELINES

ABBREVIATED VERSION

Company X seeks to select suppliers who are committed to conducting business in a very efficient, reasonable, and responsible manner. As Company X is a global force in the apparel and accessories industry today, it is important that suppliers and manufacturers conducting business with Company X remain compliant with all guidelines set forth in this document. We will not conduct business in any country where the reputation of our company would be put in jeopardy due to political, economic, or social upheaval.

SELECTION OF SUPPLIERS AND MANUFACTURERS

Company X selects suppliers and manufacturers who follow all of the set guidelines and comply with the laws and regulations of their countries.

COMMUNITY INVOLVEMENT

We will become involved in the community when opportunities arise, and we will encourage our employees to become good citizens.

EMPLOYMENT STANDARDS

We will maintain high employment standards and conduct business with only those suppliers who adhere to fair labor standards, including but not limited to compensation, safe work environment, and a workweek less than 60 hours with compensation for overtime.

CHILD LABOR

Use of workers less than 14 years of age is not allowed. We will not partner with any organization that uses child labor.

FACTORY VISITS

Buyers and other company officials who visit factories are asked to be observant of any unethical treatment of human beings and inappropriate labeling of product. They are asked to report their findings to the management so that disciplinary action can be taken.

LABELING LAWS

Company X requires that all apparel imported into the United States has correct labels in terms of care, country of origin, and content.

SIDEBAR 03.01

5. provisions on wages, usually based on local laws regarding minimum wage or prevailing wage levels in the local industry

6. provisions regarding limits on working hours, including forced overtime, in accordance with local laws

7. support for freedom of association and the right to organize collectively

As a result of this study, most of the large U.S. apparel importers have initiated a "Code of Conduct" or "Sourcing Guidelines". For examples of sourcing guidelines by major companies such as JCPenney and Levi Strauss & Co. visit the U.S. Department of Labor's Web site at www.dol.gov. Also see Sidebar 03.01 for an abbreviated version of a fake company's sourcing guidelines.

Depending on the product to be imported, there may be restrictions or taxes charged. *Quota* is a restriction or limit placed on the amount of units of a specific product a country is authorized to export or import. Either the importing or exporting country may dictate the quota. All the factories that produce the item that are affected by the quota compete for their share. If the quota capacity of a factory or country is reached, no further goods may be exported until the beginning of the next calendar year. This restriction prevents importing countries from losing business on the same type of goods being produced domestically. *Duty* is usually imposed to strengthen the price of the product and to protect consumers within the exporting country from experiencing a shortage of merchandise due to excess quantities leaving the country. Duty is a tax authorized by the customs department on a specific category of merchandise. Based on the value or type of product, a percentage rate of tax is assigned. In some countries, merchandise may qualify for reduced duty or even be duty-free depending on the trade agreement the country has with the United States. Depending on relations with some countries, goods may currently be banned for import from that country. When selecting a country for importing, it is essential to investigate any laws that apply to the product of import. While a manufacturer should be knowledgeable of any laws that affect merchandise produced in its factory, the importer should also check with an attorney or a government agency to confirm. If the supplier does not comply with the law, there may be additional fees for the importer to pay, or the foreign government may not approve the product for import. Import/export agreements are discussed in detail in Chapter 5.

It is essential to determine what port is closest to the factory and the accessibility of the port. The least expensive way to ship merchandise is by boat. The trip by water generally takes approximately two to three weeks. If merchandise is needed quickly, air shipment is an option but may be expensive depending on the weight of the shipment. Find

[handwritten note in margin: Importer is charged the duty]

Bill of Lading – shows ownership of goods
and title of goods, dates

out which shipping companies are available to transport merchandise to the port. On
what days do ships sail from the port? If a shipment is delivered to the port on Tuesday,
the container may be held up because the designated ship leaves port on Saturdays. What
is the timeline on water before the shipment reaches its destination port? What is the
estimated time to clear customs? What is the designated port of entry in the United
States, and how long might it take to travel from the port of entry to the store distribution center? The West Coast port of entry into the United States used by many exporting
countries *importers* is in Long Beach, California. Appendix B lists U.S. ports of entry.

If a retail store belongs to a buying office with an import division, the buying
office conducts research on countries for import and selects factories to produce goods.
By belonging to a buying office, stores can combine their buying power. With larger
orders placed collectively, the buying office becomes more important to the manufacturer. Larger buying groups have foreign buying offices located overseas for better control of import operations.

Macy's Merchandising Group (MMG), owned by Federated Department Stores,
operates 14 offices overseas to keep in close contact with suppliers and the overseas
market. The design, production, and product-development teams work closely
together to spot trends and design, source, and market private-label merchandise and
exclusive branded product for more than 450 stores. The two largest department store
groups, Federated and May Department Stores Company, announced a merger on
February 28, 2005, with a scheduled shareholders' meeting on July 13, 2005 to vote on
the merger. Prior to the merger, May Merchandising Group traveled overseas to
develop programs to offer to its 490-plus department stores and additional specialty
store operations throughout 46 states. For additional information, visit the Federated
Web site at www.fds.com.

Associated Merchandising Corporation (AMC), owned by Target Corporation,
offers full-service merchandising of apparel, accessories, and home furnishings for
Target Corporation and other retailers. AMC services include a fashion office responsible for identifying trends, designing product with computer-aided design and a
graphics team, developing product for private-label merchandise, and global sourcing
to seek the best country and supplier for product. The quality assurance team oversees
factory inspections and testing to be sure they comply with government laws and regulations. AMC runs a state-of-the-art information system to track merchandise shipments and inventory. The group operates more than 50 offices worldwide.

Saks Department Store Group (SDSG) operates approximately 232 department
stores, 57 Saks Fifth Avenue stores, and 52 Off 5th stores. This buying group is consid-

Country selected to import denim jeans _____

1. **Stability of the country: Discuss the status of the government, relationships with other countries, social unrest, and so on.**

2. **Conditions that may affect lead-time of production: List any natural disasters, cultural situations, and so on.**

3. **Trade organizations the country is a member of**

4. **Laws, quotas, or duties that apply to the product of import**

5. **Type of foreign currency and current exchange rate**

6. **Ports within the country and shipping companies**

7. **Suppliers within your selected country that manufacture denim jeans: Discuss the pros and cons of each supplier, and select the supplier that best suits your needs.**

FIGURE 03.01   _Perry's country analysis worksheet_

ered more upscale. For additional information, visit the Web site at www.saksincorporated.com.

Individual stores that do not belong to a buying office can contact foreign countries directly for information on products for manufacture and communicate with the government, chamber of commerce, trade associations, or banks with offices both at home and abroad. Through these contacts, the importer may learn of agents within the country who can assist with the importing process. Agents assist buyers by locating resources, communicating with the contact, negotiating price, checking for quality control, and tracking the purchase until the order ships. Determine if the agent is a sales agent who works for the manufacturer or a buying agent who will work on behalf of the buyer. Agents are paid on a commission basis. Commissions to a buying agent should be paid separately from the cost paid to the manufacturer, since it should be a separate contract. If the agent is a sales agent for the manufacturer, the commission is added to the price of the product, and duty is paid on the total price of the product, plus commission, resulting in a higher cost.

Buyers may also use domestic suppliers operating in the United States who manufacture and import merchandise from overseas for lower costs than producing domestically. Often a buyer may negotiate with a domestic vendor to purchase a shipment from its overseas factory at a reduced cost, taking control of the goods at the overseas port or port of entry close to the store. Working with a vendor in this manner allows the buyer to import product without traveling to the overseas site.

There are also trade fairs in numerous countries that buyers may attend. Many of the foreign suppliers will have a booth at the trade fair to present their merchandise. Buyers have the advantage of seeing many potential suppliers in one place who they may never have encountered searching on their own. See the CD-ROM for a list of foreign trade shows.

The *International Trade Statistics Yearbook* is another source of reference, published by the United Nations Department of Economic and Social Affairs Statistics Division. Volume I supplies details on trade by country, and volume II lists trade by commodity, providing information on 184 countries or reporting customs areas. In the United States, the Department of Treasury, U.S. Customs Service, offers the publication *Importing into the United States: A Guide for Commercial Importers* for purchase.

Using the worksheet in Figure 03.01, complete an analysis of the country from which you will import denim jeans. Refer to your country profile research in Step One as a reference.

SIMULATION: *Go to Figure 03.01 in the book or CD-ROM.*

CHAPTER 4

STEP THREE

Business Protocol
Working Across Cultures

IN THIS CHAPTER, YOU WILL LEARN:

* The importance of global communication when working across cultures
* How culture can have an effect on decision making *Jessa*
* Cultural sensitivity as it relates to conducting business
* The difference between polychronic and monochronic business cultures

Today, U.S. buyers have expanded their sources to cover, quite literally, the globe. There is no place in the world that U.S. apparel buyers do not travel to in order to obtain goods. Where the Far Eastern circuit once meant shopping the markets in Hong Kong and Taiwan for raw materials, it now also means traveling to Japan for high fashion and places such as Sri Lanka, Indonesia, Malaysia, and the Philippines for their growing number of fashion specialties. They have learned to use a global market to their advantage, molding it to current trends such as private-label manufacturing and specifications ordering. They have learned to work their way through the labyrinth of federal and international restrictions that regulate international trade.

This chapter explores the importance of working across cultures to increase the speed of the supply chain management. As you learned in Chapter 2, a garment can have up to five or more countries associated with the process of production, from a fabric supplier in China to a sewer in the Caribbean. Tracking the entire process from producer to consumer is an important part of a buyer's job today. Most of the communication takes place over the Internet, but whether a buyer is face to face or in a virtual environment, there is still the potential for cultural clashes. In this simulation you are working with the last step of the supply chain function—delivering the goods to their final destination, which is Perry's distribution center located at the flagship store in

Fredericksburg, Virginia. The logistics of moving the jeans from the manufacturer to the final destination are more commonly called *importing apparel*.

CULTURAL SENSITIVITY

Crossing cultures can be one of the most exciting experiences of anyone's life. It is important to understand cultural differences and cultural traits that can interfere when working in another country. You learned about the basic political, economical, cultural, and social traits of nations in chapter 2. Those are general traits based on culture that can interfere directly or indirectly with business communications.

Cultural sensitivity means being aware of cultural traits that differ significantly from one's own culture. Over 70 percent of all business deals taking place across cultures fail because of misunderstandings due to cultural boundaries. Ways of conducting business and cultural attitudes differ among regions of the world. One of the biggest barriers in cross-cultural communications is believing that one's culture is superior and the best. One should enter the business deal with the attitude that all cultures are different and one is not better than another.

CULTURAL ELEMENTS

Figure 04.01 lists the characteristics of a population that are considered to be elements that make up a culture.

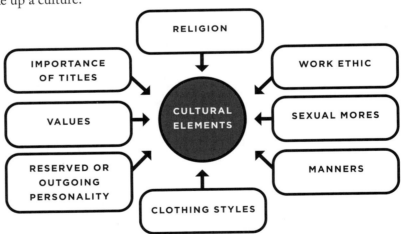

FIGURE 04.01: *Culture is a set of behaviors, beliefs, values, and traits shared by a group of people from a specific geographic area of the world. Consider the elements in this figure and how they can cause conflict when people of different cultures conduct business.*

The degrees of value individuals in a population or nation place on these elements can influence the way business is conducted. It is important to note that as a result of globalization, cultures are slowly changing. The changing cultural environment produces a domino effect that changes relationships and etiquette in the textile and apparel business.

GLOBAL COMMUNICATION

Working across several cultures at the same time can be quite challenging and can waste valuable turnaround time for garments. Table 04.01 examines the way business is conducted based on the cultural elements of each of the countries used in the model in Chapter 2. These traits need to be taken into consideration when working across cultures.

IMPORTANT CULTURAL ELEMENTS THAT AFFECT BUSINESS *Jessa*

When conducting business across cultures, it is important to be aware of cultural elements that can have an effect on business relationships.

- *Space* 2 cks

The personal space people maintain between one another differs widely among nations. On the one hand, Americans stand at arm's length from one another when they talk and feel uncomfortable if someone moves closer and invades their space. On the other hand, Asians, South Americans, and Europeans stand much closer.

- *Time* 2 cks

Punctuality is very important in the United States, Germany, Japan, and England; however, if you show up 20 minutes late to a meeting in Italy or Saudi Arabia it is acceptable and not considered rude. When conducting business in India, the person may or may not show up for a meeting.

Americans tend to schedule everything because the clock runs their entire lives—everything has a beginning and an end. They are very concerned with making the most out of the time they have and utilize every minute for something. In negotiations with other cultures, Americans are viewed as always in a hurry to make a decision. Alternatively, the Chinese take time to get to know people. You must have time and patience when conducting business in China.

TABLE 04.01

TRAITS OF NATIONS

COUNTRY	GESTURES	BUSINESS SOCIAL ETIQUETTE	GENDER ISSUES	NEGOTIATIONS
UNITED STATES	Use handshakes during first encounters	If you are invited out to lunch your host will pay.	Issues still exist with women receiving lower pay than men, but women and men can do the same jobs.	Usually the bottom line in the deal relates to financial issues. Decisions are based on subjective feelings.
CHINA	Avoid touching the Chinese; do not slap them on the back.	Usually will entertain clients with an elaborate meal and also provide female entertainment to men.	Men are almost always the decision makers.	Very cautious and will want to develop a friendship before conducting business. Business deals are based on objective and gut feelings.
HONDURAS	Very warm people; like to stand very close when speaking.	Not much entertaining, but avoid politics at all costs.	Women work in factories, but men still have control. Prefer conducting business with men.	Most people have a strong faith and will pray before they make a decision; however, the decision is well thought out and based on subjective criteria.
MEXICO	Very warm and friendly, similar to Americans.	Enjoy lunch as the main meal of the day. People will spend hours at lunch discussing business and family.	Women are taking on a more powerful role in business.	The business pace is very slow. Enjoy conversation and being friends.

JACLYN APPAREL	
I. APPEL	
Smart Time	
Emerson Road	

Divisions of Jaclyn Inc.

33 East 33rd Street
New York, NY 10016
Tel: (212) 685-6484
Fax: (212) 686-1767
bcahilljaclyn@aol.com

BRUCE CAHILL
Co-President

高 興

Jaclyn, Inc.

上 海 联 络 处

地址: 上海愚园路300号
　　申乐大厦2202室
邮编: 200040

电话: 86-21-62114889
传真: 86-21-62115401
E-mail: bcahilljaclyn@aol.com

FIGURE 04.02: *This is a business card that Bruce Cahill, copresident of Jaclyn Apparel, uses when he visits China for business. He uses a Chinese name when he is there and has it printed on his business card. Its translation is "Mr. Happy."*
SOURCE: Courtesy of Jaclyn Apparel

Another issue with time is the attitude toward the past or the future. Americans are oriented to the present and near-term future rather than to the past. Asians, South Americans, and some Europeans are both past and future oriented. The future as it relates to business success is not necessarily the focus, but rather, the future relationship between the two parties when conducting business. Most cultures appreciate and value their past histories and families more than Americans do.

When conducting business in another country, make sure your business card is printed in English on one side and the language of the country on the other. Figure 04.02 is an example of a business card printed in English on one side and Chinese on the other side.

- *Relationships*   2 exs
It is important to spend time building relationships and make an effort to build trust and rapport at all management levels. Make sure the person with whom you are building a relationship is the person who has the authority to make decisions. For more information on social and cultural elements that affect business read the article "Doing Business across Cultures" by Tammy Oaks (Sidebar 04.01).

- *Polychronic and Monochronic Cultures*   define
Anthropologist Edward Hall coined the terms ***polychronic*** for cultures that juggle many tasks at the same time and ***monochronic*** for cultures that organize single tasks

Doing Business Across Cultures

by Tammy Oaks

LONDON, England—Business-etiquette savvy is not just good sense, it can also prove to be a deal maker or breaker in today's global marketplace as more cultures interact than ever before.

Though it is impossible to fully understand all the intricacies of other societies, it is worth learning at least the basics—how to greet and address others, how to dress, how to handle business cards, personal space, eye contact, and punctuality to name a few.

First impressions are always important so showing cultural respect when greeting others is essential. In many western countries a handshake is the preferred greeting, but even differences exist there.

In Germany a firm, brief handshake with good eye contact is expected at introductions and departures while in Italy handshakes can be warm and spirited in business meetings. And in both countries it is customary to shake hands with everyone in the group upon entering and leaving, avoiding general group salutations.

Some cultures, such as the French, may kiss one another when greeting at work, but it is best to refrain from the behaviour unless they initialise it, extending your hand instead.

The Japanese often shake hands with westerners as a sign of respect and appreciate when westerners bow out of respect to their culture. Chinese may bow or shake hands.

In Saudi Arabia always shake hands with the right hand as left hands are considered unclean. Never extend your hand to a Saudi woman. And in Taiwan, western males should not initiate a hand shake with Chinese females.

Eye contact is essential in Australia, England, Germany, Italy, and the United States, for example, but it should be used with caution in Taiwan where prolonged eye contact is considered a hostile gesture.

Although time is treated differently amongst cultures, it is always in your best interest to be punctual. In Germany and Japan, arriving late is rude and unacceptable.

Don't be surprised, however, if you are kept waiting for a business meeting in Saudi Arabia, where punctuality is not of high importance.

In the U.S. and in Taiwan people are uncomfortable when their personal space is invaded, so it is recommended to stay about two arm's lengths away.

In Australia and England, an arm's length distance should be observed, while in France and Italy people may stand closer while talking.

Handle business cards in China with respect by reading it and then carefully placing it in a card case. Never place it in a shirt pocket or wallet immediately without examining it first. When distributing cards there, do so with two hands.

The safest guideline to follow for business attire is a dark suit and tie for men and a business suit or skirt and blouse for women. Avoid heavy perfumes or colognes and excessive jewelry. But it is always worth researching the attire of the country you are visiting.

Remember to wear good socks in Japan as you may be asked to remove your shoes during some business meetings.

When possible, learn a few words in the language of the country you are visiting as a sign of respect. And before you travel, contact your embassy to request briefing on business etiquette and cultural background.

SOURCE: Courtesy of CNN

SIDEBAR 04.01

TABLE 04.02

BUSINESS CHARACTERISTICS OF CULTURES

BUSINESS TRAITS	POLYCHRONIC	MONOCHRONIC
Meetings	Can be interrupted	Are hardly ever interrupted
Relationships	Very important	Not emphasized on a personal level
Status level	Usually wants to conduct business only with a high-level person in a company	Status not important; usually wants to conduct business with person who can make decisions
Eye contact	Usually does not make eye contact	Considers the person rude if eye contact is not made
Punctuality	Very flexible	Extremely important
Contracts	Hand shake is good	Expects a written contract
Deadlines	Very flexible	Not flexible

into linear sequences. While both polychronic and monochronic cultures are outcome oriented, polychronic cultures have a tendency to build relationships prior to conducting business. Monochronic cultures such as Americans, Canadians, and Germans want to make the deal as quickly as possible and move on to the next negotiation. Americans tend to focus on an agenda and complete one point at a time during a meeting, while polychronic cultures such as Asians, Latin Americans, and some Southern Europeans may focus on the entire agenda and jump around to different points throughout a meeting. They may even talk louder than Americans in an attempt to control the meeting. Table 04.02 compares polychronic and monochronic cultures.

Using the outline on the following page, create an executive summary of the culture from which you will import jeans. To complete this profile, you can draw on the resources provided in this chapter as well as http://www.culturalsavvy.com and http://www.executiveplanet.com.

SIMULATION:

Go to the business protocol worksheet on the CD-ROM.

Your executive summary should include the following information:

I. Type of culture (polychronic or monochronic)

II. Masculine or feminine (basis of culture) and gender issues

III. Negotiation style and strategies

IV. Type of communication (high-context or low-context)

V. Social and cultural elements

  A. Appropriate business dress
  B. Introductions
  C. Greetings
  D. Presentation of business cards
  E. First name or title
  F. Gestures
  G. Colors, numbers, and their meanings
  H. Space
  I. Gift giving
  J. Time
  K. Joke telling

VI. Business entertaining

  A. Proper use of utensils
  B. Table manners
  C. Alcoholic beverages
  D. Appropriate conversation subjects

CHAPTER 5

STEP FOUR

Importing Trade Agreements and Laws

Policies, Laws, and Trade Agreements
Governing the Importation of Textiles and Apparel

IN THIS CHAPTER, YOU WILL LEARN:

* The impact of globalization on textile and apparel trade
* The historical perspective on the textile and apparel trade
* A few basic trade fundamentals
* Important trade agreements between the United States and countries around the world
* Relevant importing laws enforced by the U. S. Customs Border Protection Agency

THE IMPACT OF GLOBALIZATION ON TEXTILE AND APPAREL TRADE

The United States has had a love-hate relationship with trade liberalization throughout history, balancing domestic needs with global growth. Retailers and importers favor trade agreements with liberal rules of origin and sharp duty reductions. The domestic textile industry, however, opposes most free-trade pacts and fights for tight restrictions, such as requiring countries to use U.S. yarn and fabric in negotiations. There might not be much of a consensus on free-trade agreements, but all agree that trade pacts and liberalization have changed the face of textile and apparel commerce (*WWD* 2002).

The textile and apparel industry has contributed significantly to the globalization of many national economies. The international arena promotes an environment where textile and apparel trade occurs daily around the world. The raw material of a garment is bought in one country, shipped thousands of miles for processing, moved thousands of miles to be turned into a garment, and moved thousands of miles to be sold. These transactions to get the product produced and sold involve international business. Think of all the nations, labor, machinery, laws, and decisions that have to go into the actual creation of a product. Countries around the world are dependent upon the movement and production of fashion apparel to contribute to their economies. When a country is building or maintaining its economy, the principles of economics apply. The principles of economics are based on the following three choices:

1. What goods should be produced?

2. How should the goods be produced?

3. For whom should the goods be produced?

The manner in which all nations choose to use their resources, labor, and capital does not change from country to country.

Most of the economies around the world today are considered mixed economies, which means they have both government and privately owned businesses. People are free to make decisions about what they want to buy and where they want to work. As discussed earlier, in the newly industrialized countries and less-developed countries, industry is limited. As U.S. textile and apparel manufacturers have moved offshore into foreign countries, the industry has contributed to global economic growth. While some countries are just at the beginning of their industrial revolutions, the United States is at the beginning of its technological revolution. Countries at either of these stages complement each other by helping to move textiles and apparel faster and more efficiently and in turn contributing to the world economy.

With the onset of globalization, nations around the world have encouraged global trade, but at the same time they have protected industries within their home territories from competition abroad. This chapter focuses on basic trade fundamentals, the historical perspectives of textile and apparel trade, and trade agreements and laws relevant to importing textiles and apparel into the United States.

BASIC TRADE FUNDAMENTALS

Trade activities have two basic partners: the seller and the buyer. As you know, textiles and apparel bought in another country are called *imports* and products sold to another country are called *exports*.

Obstacles, or *trade barriers*, arise from importing and exporting. Trade barriers can exist in the forms of culture, communication, and laws. The most common barrier to trade is a tariff or duty (tax) put on imported goods. Tariffs raise the cost of an item and can discourage companies from buying or producing textiles and apparel in coun-

TABLE 05.01

TYPES OF TARIFFS

TARIFF	DEFINITION	PRODUCT	VALUE	TARIFF	TOTAL VALUE
Ad valorem	Percentage of the value of the good	Men's jacket	$25	16%	$29
Specific	Set dollar amount	Men's jacket	$25	$10	$35
Combination	Percentage of value plus a set dollar amount	Men's jacket	$25	16% plus $10	$39

tries in which they have to pay these tariffs. As illustrated in Table 05.01 there are three basic types of tariffs used today: ad valorem, specific, or a combination. An ***ad valorem tariff*** is used when a percentage of the value of an item is added to each product. A ***specific tariff*** is a set dollar amount added to each product. The ***combination tariff*** is when both ad valorem and specific tariffs are applied. The example in Table 05.01 shows the differences in total value depending on the tariff rate used.

A quota, which limits the number of goods that may be imported into a country during a certain period of time, is another type of barrier. Quotas and their elimination will be discussed later in the chapter.

Free trade, which is the process of conducting business without any barriers, is the driving force of globalization. Free-trade zones have emerged throughout the world. These areas are usually located near ports and manufacturing plants that can store textile and apparel items without tariffs being applied. These goods have either been imported for the purposes of storing or reshipping to final destinations.

Balance of trade is a measure used by countries to determine what a country imports and exports. Balance of trade is the difference between what a country exports and what it imports. If a country imports more than it exports it is considered to have a trade deficit. If the country exports more than it imports it is considered to have a trade surplus. The ideal situation is to have exports and imports equal with each other. Balancing trade can be a difficult task for a country. Figure 05.01 shows that the United States imports more than it exports, so overall a trade deficit exists. As a result of the difficulty of balancing trade, trade initiatives have been developed to both encourage and discourage trade.

Understanding these initiatives can have a tremendous effect on the duty of the garment being imported into the United States. In some situations, manufacturing in a

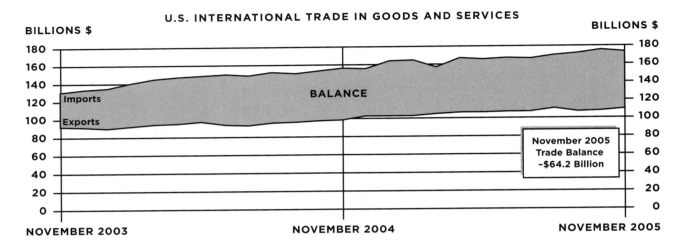

U.S. INTERNATIONAL TRADE IN GOODS AND SERVICES

FIGURE 05.01 *This chart shows how much the U.S. trade deficit has grown from November 2003 to November 2005. There is an increase in imports and a slight increase in exports.*

SOURCE: U.S. Census Bureau

particular country can delete the duty altogether; therefore, it is advantageous for manufacturers or retailers to seek the lowest duty cost because this can lower the retail price of the garment.

HISTORICAL PERSPECTIVE OF TEXTILE AND APPAREL TRADE

Fifty-two countries were involved in the ***Multi-Fiber Arrangement (MFA)***, a trade agreement designed to control import penetration from newly industrialized countries to developed countries. Import quotas were created so that a country could not have a monopoly on any textile items. This agreement provided an arena whereby free trade could exist among member countries. The quotas have decreased annually for those countries belonging to the ***World Trade Organization***, which at the time of this writing is a watchdog for MFA. Quotas were eliminated January 2005.

There is a lot of dissention around the world because China is predicted to become a dominant player in the production of textiles and apparel, setting the stage for an open market, which would eventually hurt less-developed countries that are not in a position to compete. Many textile and apparel associations in the United States

TABLE 05.02

FOUR STEPS USED TO FREE TEXTILES AND APPAREL FROM IMPORT QUOTAS

STEP	PERCENTAGE OF PRODUCTS TO BE BROUGHT UNDER GATT (INCLUDING REMOVAL OF ANY QUOTAS)	PERCENTAGE OF PRODUCTS TO BE BROUGHT UNDER GATT (INCLUDING REMOVAL OF ANY QUOTAS)
STEP 1 January 1995– December 1997	16% (minimum, taking 1990 imports as base)	6.9% per year
STEP 2 January 1998– December 2001	17%	8.7% per year
STEP 3 January 2002– December 2004	18%	11.05% per year
STEP 4 January 2005	49%	No quota left

The example is based on the commonly used 6 percent annual expansion rate of the old Multi-Fiber Arrangement.

In practice, the rates used under the MFA vary from product to product.

SOURCE: World Trade Organization

have proposed to Congress that quotas be placed on specific imports as safeguards to protect them from Chinese competition.

The first international approach to controlling trade was the formation of the *General Agreement on Tariffs and Trade*, better know as GATT. This was a world effort led by the United States to help solve and control international trade obstacles. In essence, this agreement established international rules for trade. There were many countries that attempted to restrict textile and apparel imports for the purposes of protecting their own products. This atmosphere created a need for control of imports and the MFA evolved (Table 05.02).

Table 05.02 is from the WTO Web site. It shows the steps in GATT designed to delete the quotas on textiles and apparel.

International trade agreements and treaties are designed to promote free trade and/or reduce trade barriers among the United States and other countries. The following trade agreements and treaties have components that help reduce trade barriers when importing textiles and apparel in the United States and other countries.

Generalized System of Preferences (GSP)

Twenty-five developed countries, mainly located in the Northern Hemisphere, created the **Organization for Economic Cooperation and Development (OECD)** in 1961. The principle behind the creation of the OECD was to promote social and economic growth among the countries as well as to help developing countries by assisting them with trade issues.

The **Generalized System of Preferences (GSP)** grew out of the OECD to help promote exports from developing countries by allowing them tariff preferences. Once a country reaches "developed country" status it no longer needs duty preferences. Examples of countries that no longer qualify under GSP are Taiwan, Hong Kong, and South Korea.

There are currently 150 countries that fall under the GSP. This is the most widely used trade agreement. The product being imported from one of the GSP countries into the United States must meet the follow criteria:

* Product must be shipped directly from the country

* 35 percent of the product's appraised value by U.S. Customs must have been added in the country

EXAMPLE

If the appraised value of a cashmere coat is $2,000, 35 percent of the value must have occurred in a GSP for the tariff duty to be comparatively low.

Cut in the United Stated	$1,300
Shipped to Philippines where it was sewn	$ 700
Total value of the coat	$2,000

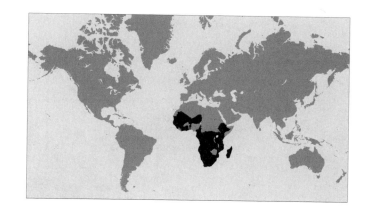

FIGURE 05.02:

Countries involved in the African Growth and Opportunity Act

SOURCE: Courtesy of Theresa Engle

Andean Pact

The ***Andean Pact*** is a comprehensive trade bill passed on November 3, 2002. Apparel imported into the United States from Colombia, Ecuador, Bolivia, and Peru are duty-free only if textiles used in the production of the apparel are from the United States. Shipments are limited to a quota of 2 percent a year. After 2006, the limits will be raised to 5 percent per year but the trade breaks must be renewed.

African Growth and Opportunity Act (AGOA)

The ***African Growth and Opportunity Act (AGOA)*** was signed into law on May 18, 2000. It is part of The Trade and Development Act of 2000. The act offers incentives for African countries to continue their efforts to open economies and build free markets. AGOA provides reforming African countries with the most liberal access to the U.S. market available to any country or region with which the United States does not have a free trade agreement (www.agoa.gov).

Some of the countries in Africa that are encouraged to take advantage or already taking advantage of AGOA benefits include Angola, Cape Verde, Chad, Ghana, Kenya, Madagascar, Mauritius, Mozambique, Nigeria, South Africa, and Uganda. Figure 05.02 gives a geographical look at the countries involved in the African Growth and Opportunity Act.

Under AGOA, apparel made in eligible countries from sub-Saharan Africa from U.S. fabric, yarn, and thread are duty-free and quota-free. Lesser-developed countries such as Botswana and Namibia and almost 30 other countries are eligible for duty-free export from fabric originating anywhere in the world. This is an exception because their per capita GNP is below $1,500.

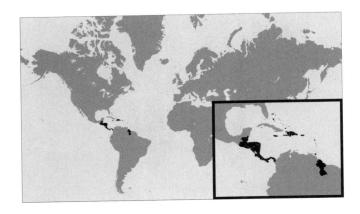

FIGURE 05.03:
*Countries involved in the
Caribbean Basin Initiative*
SOURCE: Courtesy of Theresa Engle

Caribbean Basin Trade Preference Act

The **Caribbean Basin Initiative**, or CBI, is a general term used to refer to the Caribbean Basin Economic Recovery Act of 1983 (CBERA), the Caribbean Basin Economic Recovery Expansion Act of 1990 (CBERA Expansion Act), and the U.S. **Caribbean Basin Trade Partnership Act** of 2000 (CBTPA), collectively (http://ustr.gov/Trade_Development/Preference_Programs/CBI/section_Index.html).

Initially the CBI was developed to promote economic development in the Caribbean Islands. This area of the world is considered to be a nontraditional area for business; therefore, incentives to help these countries have benefited the textile and apparel industry by allowing duty-free entry to the United States for products manufactured in countries classified as CBI. Other elements of the program have indirectly helped the textile and apparel industry by providing U.S. government special programs for textiles and apparel through various trade agreements.

The countries that benefit from the CBI include Antiqua, Aruba, the Bahamas, Barbados, Belize, British Virgin Islands, Costa Rica, Dominica, Dominican Republic, El Salvador, Grenada, Guatemala, Guyana, Haiti, Honduras, Jamaica, Montserrat, Netherlands Antilles, Nicaragua, Panama, St. Kitts and Nevis, St. Lucia, St. Vincent & the Grenadines, and Trinidad and Tobago. Figure 05.03 gives a geographical look at the countries included in the CBI.

The CBERA was enacted to extend the CBI, which was going to expire in 1995. Under this act leather was added with provisions to become a duty-free good. It also allows for the rules of origin to be altered by the president of the United States, making products produced in CBI countries (which means that the product must be imported directly from a CBI country into U.S. Customs territory) conform to transformation requirements and have at least 35 percent value added to the garment.

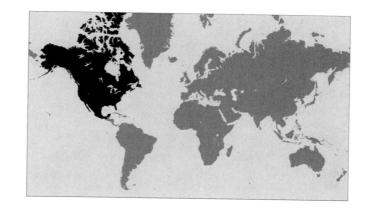

FIGURE 05.04:

*Countries involved in
the North American
Free Trade Agreement*

SOURCE: Courtesy of Theresa Engle

The CBTA provides even more in-depth and advantageous benefits in the area of textiles and apparel. The act specifically states that garments are exempt from duty if they meet the following:

* Assembled from fabrics made and cut in the United States, manufactured from U.S. yarn entered under HT9802.00.08 or in Harmonized Tariff Schedule Chapter 61 and 62 (which allows for certain processes such as embroidery and stone washing). You may refer to the HTS Chapter 62 in the CD-ROM for more information.

* Cut and assembled from U.S. fabric, made with U.S. yarn, sewn in CBPTA countries with U.S.-formed thread.

* Knit to shape (other than certain socks) from U.S. yarns, and knit apparel cut and wholly assembled from fabric formed in one or more beneficiary countries or in the United States, from U.S. yarns, with certain caps attached (www.mac. doc.gov).

CBTPA will remain in force until September 20, 2008 or another free trade agreement is enacted, whichever comes first.

North American Free Trade Agreement

On December 17, 1992, President George H. W. Bush signed the **North American Free Trade Agreement (NAFTA)**. This agreement eliminated trade barriers between Canada, the United States, and Mexico, thereby creating a free trade area. Figure 05.04 gives a geographical look at the countries involved in the North American Free Trade Agreement. The facilitation of the agreement enabled textiles and apparel to be imported and exported among these countries duty- and quota-free.

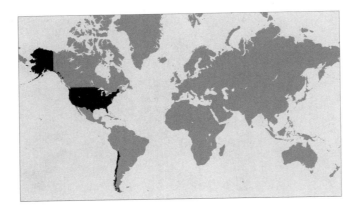

FIGURE 05.05:
*Countries involved in
the United States–Chile
Free Trade Agreement*
SOURCE: Courtesy of Theresa Engle

United States–Chile Free Trade Agreement (U.S.–CFTA)

On September 3, 2003, the **United States–Chile Free Trade Agreement (U.S.–CFTA)** was signed, and it was implemented on January 1, 2004. Trade between these two countries is basically duty- and quota-free but restrictions apply for textiles and apparel, including:

* Yarn must originate in Chile or the United States

* Fabric must originate in Chile or the United States

* Apparel yarn used in production must originate in Chile or the United States

Other fabrics or goods originating outside these countries are given a tariff preference level (TPL), which means that the good is not totally duty-free. Also, goods that are given the classification of preferential tariff treatment are not subject to merchandise processing fees and harbor maintenance fees, which are usually included in the shipping costs when importing a product. Figure 05.05 gives a geographical look at the countries involved in the United States–Chile Free Trade Agreement.

United States–Singapore Free Trade Agreement (U.S.–SFTA)

The **United States–Singapore Free Trade Agreement** was signed on the same day as the U.S.–CFTA: September 3, 2003. Textiles and apparel and must meet the requirements of the agreement to qualify as originating goods. The requirements are the same as stated in the U.S.–CFTA (see above requirements under U.S.–CFTA) and both agreements are based on requirements similar to NAFTA. Figure 05.06 gives a geographical look at the countries involved in the United States–Singapore Free Trade Agreement.

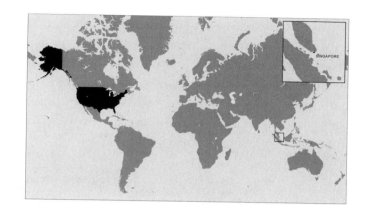

FIGURE 05.06:
Countries involved in the United States–Singapore Free Trade Agreement
SOURCE: Courtesy of Theresa Engle

United States–Central America–Dominican Republic Free Trade Agreement (CAFTA–DR)
The **United States–Central America–Dominican Republic Free Trade Agreement** was signed by President George W. Bush on August 5, 2004. This agreement is designed to eliminate trade barriers and tariffs and to expand regional opportunities. This agreement is among the United States, Costa Rica, Dominican Republic, Guatemala, and El Salvador. These countries are currently importing apparel duty-free under the Caribbean Basin Initiative, Generalized System of Preferences, and Most-Favored Nation programs.

LAWS AND PROVISIONS

Sometimes countries set prices extremely low for foreign trade. This type of pricing benefits the customer, but it is illegal. A manufacturer may **dump** a product to drive the competition out of business. They would then attempt to regain the market and reprice the goods, thereby creating a monopoly on the product. Countries have adopted antidumping laws or antidumping tariffs to prevent these situations. If a manufacturer is thought to be dumping his or her product, the U.S. industry may file a complaint to the International Trade Administration (ITA). The ITA may order an additional duty amount to create fair competition among producers.

In many countries the government will subsidize a particular industry through grants or cash advances. This can create an unfair advantage for the foreign product. A countervailing duty is imposed to create an even playing field for all imports receiving government subsidies.

SIMULATION:
*Go to the import-
ing trade agree-
ments, laws, and
policies worksheet
on the CD-ROM
and the Helpful
Web Site Resources
in the book or on
the CD-ROM.*

As a buyer, you must understand all laws and trade agreements that will affect importing jeans into the United States. Conduct in-depth research about specific trade agreements and laws that impact the importation of jeans. Under the "Agencies, Associations, and Organizations" and "Economics and Statistical Information" sections of the Helpful Web Site Resources, you will find Web sites that can help you begin your research. You need to use at least five resources. Write a five-page paper using the following outline as a guide:

PART I   State and define the trade agreement specific to your country.

PART II   List and define the laws of the United States that importers must follow when importing jeans.

CHAPTER 6

STEP FIVE

Classifying the Import Product

Resources Available for Importers

IN THIS CHAPTER, YOU WILL LEARN:

---

* Resources that are available to assist importers
* Importing regulations associated with the textile and apparel industry
* How to classify an import using the Harmonized Tariff Schedule

---

Importing goods into the United States is an extremely difficult process. Every good that is imported into the United States is affected by its own circumstances and requires specialized knowledge about specific facts. An importer must comply and follow laws and regulations that have been put in place by the U.S. government. It is the U.S. Customs and Border Patrol's responsibility to monitor and make sure all laws are being obeyed by businesses importing goods.

A tremendous amount of resources are available to aid importers, ranging from private consultants to government publications. This chapter focuses on the resources available to assist importers, the regulations that must be followed, and the information on how to classify a product using the Harmonized Tariff Schedule.

RESOURCES AVAILABLE TO ASSIST THE IMPORTER

A *customs broker* is an intermediary who assists businesses large and small with the process of moving goods through Customs. They are generally licensed in the countries in which they work. Their most important job is to know all importing rules and regulations. They must also be very familiar with the Customs Modernization Act, which was designed to streamline and automate the importation process. The legal responsibility for knowing and adhering to laws and regulations, classifying goods, and paying appropriate duty rates rests with the importer.

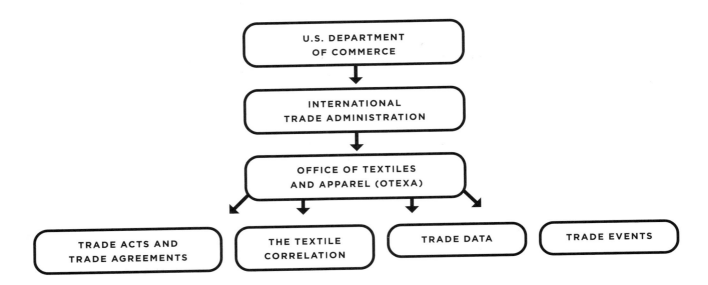

FIGURE 06.01: *This flow chart shows the organization of the governing bodies of trade in the United States. The Office of Textiles and Apparel (OTEXA) is specifically designed to help importers and exporters who work with textiles and apparel.*

It is important to understand how the governing bodies of trade are organized. Figure 06.01 shows the organization of governing bodies of trade for the United States. They help implement the trade agreements that the U.S. Congress has passed as laws. **The Office of Textiles and Apparel (OTEXA)** monitors and guides trade-related issues and functions in the textile and apparel sector. It employs many trade specialists who act as consultants and answer questions regarding importing and exporting.

The International Trade Administration (ITA) is designed to help U.S. businesses participate in international trade. The ITA acts as a watchdog for unfair competition from abroad such as dumped and subsidized imports. Although it is not a direct resource for importers, it acts as a protector for them. It is important to understand its units and the purpose of each one (Table 06.01). Table 06.01 lists the administrative units within the ITA and the responsibility of each unit.

Trade Associations exist to help importers and other professionals in the textile and apparel industry. They are designed to keep abreast of all new laws, research, and trade agreements. The American Apparel and Footwear Association is one of the largest associations (Figure 06.02). It keeps track of all statistical data related to

TABLE 06.01

INTERNATIONAL TRADE ADMINISTRATION UNITS

The commercial service	Helps businesses who are producing in other countries or selling to markets in other countries. Commercial offices are located throughout the world.
Trade development	Helps to identify markets for specific products.
Market access and compliance	Helps businesses identify trade opportunities for specific products
Import administration	Ensures that trade agreements are enforced to create a fair playing field in the domestic marketplace for importers.

importing and exporting apparel and footwear. It also lobbies before Congress for laws and policies that affect trade. The following is a list of trade organizations and their addresses:

American Apparel and Footwear Association
1601 N. Kent Street, Suite 1200
Arlington, VA 22209
1-800-520-2262
www.apparelandfootwear.org

International Association of Clothing Designers and Executives
475 Park Avenue South
New York, NY 10016
www.iacde.com

National Association of Men's Sportswear Buyers (NAMSB)
60 East 42nd Street
New York, NY 10165
www.namsb.com

FIGURE 06.02: *AAFA executives and staff gather in front of the White House before meeting with Assistant to the President on Legislative Affairs David Hobbs in the West Wing.* (LEFT TO RIGHT) FRONT ROW: *Gerald Evans, Sara Lee Branded Apparel; AAFA President & CEO Kevin Burke; Bernie Leifer, S. G. Footwear; David Martino, Russell-Newman, Inc.; AAFA Chairman Ed Emma, Jockey International; Peter Gabbe, Carole Hochman Designs, Inc.; AAFA GR Representative Carey McCombie.* BACK ROW: *Paul Charron, Liz Claiborne Inc.; Jerry Cook, Sara Lee Branded Apparel; Jim Jacobsen, Kellwood Co.; Charlie Komar, Charles Komar & Sons, Inc.; Joe Hollander, AC/Automated Components; Peter Boneparth, Jones Apparel Group; AAFA Senior VP Steve Lamar; Charlie Gilbert, Charles Gilbert Associates, Inc.*
SOURCE: Provided by the American Apparel and Footwear Association (AAFA) © 2005.

National Textile Association
6 Beacon Street
Boston, MA 02108
www.nationaltextile.org

United States Association of Importers of Textile and Apparel
13 East 16th Street
New York, NY 10003
www.usaita.com

Trade publications are published for professionals in the textile and apparel industry. These publications are designed to target specific sectors such as men's, women's, and children's markets as well as the people who work in the logistics of moving products. Included in these publications are articles that contain information about sourcing, importing, exporting, logistics, trends, and other relevant information that can help with the importation process. The following is a list of trade publications for importers:

Apparel Magazine is published monthly and includes information for supply chain managers, including manufacturing, sourcing, and technical information.

Daily News Record (DNR) is published weekly by Fairchild Publications and targets the menswear industry. News articles focus on both domestic and international subjects.

Journal of Commerce is published monthly. Included in the subscription rate is access to their Web site. It covers logistics, transportation issues, customs, and cargo, and the Web site has industry links.

Women's Wear Daily (WWD) is a daily (except weekends) newspaper published by Fairchild Publications. It provides information on the women's segment, including apparel, accessories, legwear, and beauty. News articles focus on both domestic and international subjects.

Trade clubs are organizations located in many cities throughout the United States. The clubs consist mostly of importers, exporters, custom agents, and freight forwarders. The main purpose of these clubs is for the members to network with one another. Usually they are nonprofit organizations and their main mission is to educate and help one another in business.

Supply chain management companies are becoming very popular. Businesses can simply hire them to design, source, produce, and import their products for a fee.

Import training seminars are offered by a variety of experts. Many firms offer assistance and training online.

Textile and apparel consultants are sources of information for existing businesses and start-ups. They provide services, research, trend forecasting, and much more for textile, retail, and wholesale product companies. Infomat.com is a fashion Web site designed as an information resource for the global fashion industry, suppliers, retailers, and designers (Figure 06.03).

Find...

Associations • Catalogs • Contractors • Designers
Executives • Importers • Jobbers • Manufacturers
Notions & Trim • Research • Sales Leads • Sales
Reps Showrooms • Trade shows • Wholesalers

Just what you've been searching for!

Only one search engine and information service
delivers the global fashion industry categorized and
organized into a FREE, easy-to-use rolodex and comprehensive guide. If you are a textile, apparel or
accessories professional www.infomat.com is the
address you need to know. Our proprietary search
and filtering technology lets you find sales leads,
source, get research, find reps, browse catalogs,
calendars and more.

Call 212-398-5505
or visit
www.infomat.com

infomat
Fashion Industry Information Services
and Search Engine since 1998.

FIGURE 06.03: *This ad from infomat.com advertises its services to the retail and wholesale textile and apparel industry. An importer may consult with infomat to secure a list of denim manufacturers in a particular country.*
SOURCE: Courtesy of Infomat

REGULATIONS ASSOCIATED WITH THE TEXTILE AND APPAREL INDUSTRY

Today, the most important regulation with which to comply when importing into the United States is the Customs Modernization Act, as mentioned earlier in the chapter. Noncompliance results in delays in shipments, which can have an adverse effect on the inventory of a retail store. Retailers cannot sell goods if they are being held up in a warehouse somewhere because they didn't have the proper documentation to clear Customs. Not keeping proper documentation can result in fines from $1,000 to $100,000. All necessary paperwork must be kept on file for a period of five years by the importer. Under the Modernization Act, paperwork can be saved electronically; it is no longer necessary to keep hard copies if you do archive in your computer's hard drive.

CLASSIFICATION OF TEXTILES AND APPAREL

According to the e-book by Sandra L. Tumbarello, Import Basics, "Quick Start" Guide, the most common classification error importers make is usually identified during audits by U.S. Customs. Auditing is done to make sure the product being imported has the correct value so that the correct amount of duty has been imposed. The correct duty also comes from correct classification of the product. For example, if a $10 shirt was made in Mexico and imported into the United States no duty would be charged under NAFTA. However, if the $10 shirt was produced in China a 60-cent duty would be charged and the value of the shirt would be $10.60. An importer has to have the correct knowledge or at least access to information that will ensure correct classification. A helpful resource is *Customs Valuation Encyclopedia*, and it may be purchased at bookstores or online. It contains many examples of valuing products and it is especially helpful for first-time importers.

According to the U.S. Rules of Origin published May 1998 and revised May 2004 by the U.S. Customs and Border Protection, country-of-origin marking rules must be followed. Identifying the country of origin also helps with determining classification. There are two basic rules of origin: non-preferential and preferential. Non-preferential is when there is no trade agreement to apply to the production and importation of a product. Preferential treatment is applied to merchandise produced under various trade agreements.

A Certificate of Origin is a document used for all products and filed with Customs to let them know where the product originated. Textiles and apparel have their own rules for country of origin. The publication U.S. Rules of Origin for Textiles and Apparel Products published by U.S. Customs can be found on the CD-ROM.

The ***Harmonized Tariff Schedule (HTS)*** is a book used by importers to classify their product numerically as well as descriptively. The book, which can also be accessed online, provides tariff rates and statistical categories for all merchandise imported into the United States.

The description of the product is always listed on the invoice, which is a form used in the importing process. From this description an importer is usually able to look up the classification in the HTS. Apparel is one of the more complex products to classify because there are so many variables that are used in production. Fiber content, whether it is knit or woven, and the name of the garment are useful characteristics to use when describing the apparel.

The HTS is organized by chapter, beginning with Chapter 1, which consists of live animals and animal products, and ending with Chapter 99, which covers categories of special products that may be temporarily imported for repair or alteration. The HTS is published as a book as well as online at www.usitc.gov. It is printed annually and periodically updated online.

Chapter 62 of the HTS, "Articles of Apparel and Clothing Accessories, Not Knitted or Crocheted," can be found on the CD-ROM. See Figure 06.04 for an example of a page from the HTS.

Harmonized Tariff Schedule of the United States (2005)
Annotated for Statistical Reporting Purposes

Heading/ Subheading	Stat. Suf- fix	Article Description	Unit of Quantity	Rates of Duty		
				1		2
				General	Special	
6101		Men's or boys' overcoats, carcoats, capes, cloaks, anoraks (including ski-jackets), windbreakers and similar articles, knitted or crocheted, other than those of heading 6103:				
6101.10.00	00	Of wool or fine animal hair (434)	doz. kg	61.7¢/kg + 16%	Free (CA,CL,IL, JO,MX,SG) 15.5% (AU)	77.2¢/kg + 54.5%
6101.20.00		Of cotton	. . . .	15.9%	Free (CA,CL,IL, JO,MX,SG) 15.5% (AU)	50%
	10	Men's (334)	doz. kg			
	20	Boys' (334)	doz. kg			
6101.30 6101.30.10	00	Of man-made fibers: Containing 25 percent or more by weight of leather (634)	doz. kg	5.6%	Free (CA,CL,IL,JO, MX,SG) 5% (AU)	35%
6101.30.15	00	Other: Containing 23 percent or more by weight of wool or fine animal hair (434)	doz. kg	38.6¢/kg + 10%	Free (CA,CL,IL, JO,MX,SG) 9.8% (AU)	77.2¢/kg + 54.5%
6101.30.20		Other	. . . .	28.2%	Free (CA,CL,IL, MX,SG) 15.5% (AU) 14.4% (JO)	72%
	10	Men's (634)	doz. kg			
	20	Boys' (634)	doz. kg			
6101.90 6101.90.10	00	Of other textile materials: Containing 70 percent or more by weight of silk or silk waste (734)	doz. kg	0.9%	Free (AU,CA,CL, E,IL,J, JO,MX,SG)	45%
6101.90.90		Other	. . . .	5.7%	Free (CA,CL,E*,IL, JO,MX,SG) 5.1% (AU)	45%
	10	Subject to cotton restraints (334)	doz. kg			
	20	Subject to wool restraints (434)	doz. kg			
	30	Subject to man-made fiber restraints (634)	doz. kg			
	60	Other (834)	doz. kg			

FIGURE 06.04: *This is a typical page from the Harmonized Tariff Schedule of the United States, which importers use to look up the duty rate on products. A buyer may look up a boy's overcoat made of cotton. If the coat is made in China, the duty is 15.9%, but if it is made in Mexico, it is duty-free.*

SOURCE: International Trade Data System

In the first column of Figure 06.04, you will see several ten-digit numbers. Every product entering the United States is classified using one of these HTS numbers. The breakdown of the ten-digit harmonized number can be found on the Web site listed on page 71.

Your next step in the importing simulation is to find the correct harmonized tariff number using the Harmonized Tariff Schedule. Below are the abbreviated steps that you should follow to classify a product.

STEP #1 Determine which heading applies—refer to both the heading text (the text that appears in the tariff next to the four-digit heading number) and the legal notes. The legal notes are at the beginning of the section in Figure 06.04; the example is from section XI. You may refer to the Web site to find the legal notes at the beginning of the section. This will give you the first four digits of the number.

STEP #2 Determine the subheading and the condition within the subheading. Once you have steps one and two with the heading and subheading, you can determine the rate of duty.

Figure 06.04 shows how the pages from the HTS are in outline form, the last three columns, titled General, Special, and, 2, are used to determine the rate of duty. The General duty column applies U.S. normal trade relations duty rates. The Special column applies to countries with which the United States has preferential trade programs, such as NAFTA, and where the tariff is reduced or null. Column 2 applies to countries for which very specific trade relations are being enforced by the U.S. government such as trade embargoes, antidumping duties, and countervailing duties.

Using the HTS, determine the classification number. Explain your reasons for using the number. Refer to the abbreviated HTS located on your CD-ROM to determine the classification number, but first you will have to conduct research to figure out the classification process an importer must perform to get the correct number.

SIMULATION: *Go to the classifying the product worksheet and Chapter 62 of the HTS on the CD-ROM.*

CHAPTER 7

STEP SIX

The Cost Sheet

Financing Your Import

IN THIS CHAPTER, YOU WILL LEARN:

* What factors determine the cost of a garment
* How to estimate costs to produce and import a product
* Where to research duty and quota information for a classification or product
* What forms of payment are accepted when importing merchandise

A combination of factors determines the cost of producing an article of clothing. These factors include fabric, cut, make, and trim, as well as logistics and transportation. Table 07.01 divides these into three separate categories. Compare the categories by percentages of total cost. Discuss which factors are somewhat fixed and which factors give buyers more flexibility.

TABLE 07.01

COST FACTORS FOR APPAREL PRODUCTION	
Fabric	40–50%
Cut, make, and trim (CMT)	20–30%
Labor percentage of CMT	15–20%
Trim percentage of CMT	5–10%
Logistics and transportation	30–40%
Total costs	100%

FABRIC COST

The greatest expense is the cost of the fabric, which is generally 40 to 50 percent or more of the total cost. The price of fabric varies based on its fiber and quality. A buyer selects fabric based on the classification of merchandise, target retail price point for each item, function of the merchandise, seasonality of the product, availability of fabric, and factory production capability. All costs contributing to the total cost of the product are listed on a cost sheet to determine expenses and pricing.

To produce a single classification, such as denim jeans, only one type of fabric is required. If there will be a collection of apparel, more consideration is given to selecting fabrics that coordinate and may have similar design aspects. For example, a summer tropical theme would include lightweight fabrics. Pants, skirts, and jackets might be a solid fabric offered in several colors. Blouses and tops in novelty patterns of palm trees, beach scenes, and tropical drinks would have background colors matching or coordinating with the solid pieces. Factories contracted to cut and sew the garment may source the fabric for the buyer, or the buyer may source the fabric from a different supplier and ship to the factory producing the merchandise, depending on the cost and availability of fabric within the region where goods will be produced. The higher the quality of a fabric, the higher its cost. Knowing the target retail price of a garment provides the buyer with an idea of the allowance for fabric cost. For example, a pair of denim jeans is targeted to retail for $48. If the desired margin is 60 percent, the landed cost estimate is $19.20 for a pair of jeans, or 40 percent of the retail. One half, or 50 percent, of the landed cost is $9.60, the dollar amount estimated for fabric cost per item. Buyers select colors and patterns of fabric from swatches shown of existing offerings, or, the buyer may request to have fabric dyed to a specific color or design an exclusive pattern. Special requests more than likely will have higher yardage minimum requirements and cost more. Fabric is purchased by the total yardage needed for production. When pattern pieces are cut from the yardage, there will be some fallout, or wasted fabric, between the pattern pieces. It is difficult to estimate fabric costs for a single item due to fallout, the fact that smaller size garments use less fabric than larger sizes, and the minimum order quantity of fabric required for purchase.

CUT, MAKE, AND TRIM

Cut, make, and trim costs include all the steps of the production process, the direct labor and factory overhead costs for production, and the trim needed to complete the garment. Cut, make, and trim accounts for approximately 20 to 30 percent of the total cost of the product. An estimated 15 to 20 percent represents labor costs, with the remaining 5 to 10 percent accounting for trim. The more difficult the style of the design, the higher the labor costs will be. Buyers must consider the complexity of design when sourcing fabric. If a design is more complicated, a lower price fabric may be selected to offset the higher labor costs. The reverse is also true. If a design is simple to make, the dollar amount allotted for fabric may increase. Initial labor costs may include designing and grading the pattern, making samples of the product for approval, and making the marker, or pattern layout, of all sizes. Production labor costs include spreading the layers of fabric, laying the marker, cutting the pattern pieces, sewing the garment, applying special finishes, pressing, and packaging. Additional costs to cover administrative expenses and profit are added to the total cost to produce the item.

Trim includes buttons, zippers, thread, snaps, hooks, and other findings such as braid, cording, lace, elastic, and beading. Trim and findings are purchased by the yard, gross, or dozen but are listed on the cost sheet by unit price for costing purposes. The trim grouping also includes product and care labels, hangtags, price ticketing for customers, and packaging.

LOGISTICS AND TRANSPORTATION COSTS

The remaining costs to produce the item include transportation and shipping charges to transport the merchandise from the foreign port to the United States, in addition to duty charges. Often the factory will include the transportation cost from the factory to the foreign port of export in their price quote.

The least expensive method of shipping is by sea, in containers that are 20 feet, 40 feet, and 45 feet in size. Containers are loaded onto boats or barges and transported to the receiving port of entry. The total cubic feet needed to fill a container is used to calculate shipping charges from the foreign port to the United States port of entry. If a container is not filled, *less-than-container-load (LCL)* charges may apply. Buyers will often have a *consolidator* combine shipments for the store from various factories so they can fill a container. The most common container size is 40 feet and holds approximately 2,200 cubic feet of cartons. Table 07.02 lists freight charges negotiated by a manufacturer from various Asian ports to Long Beach, California, one of the main U.S. ports. The total dollar amount charged to transport the container from the foreign port to the United States applies whether the container is full or not. If there are 3,600 garments in a 40-foot container traveling from Hong Kong to Long Beach, the cost of

TABLE 07.02

INBOUND CONTAINER FREIGHT COSTS FROM
ASIAN ORIGIN PORT TO LONG BEACH, CALIFORNIA

PORT	20'	40'	40'HC	45'
Busan	$2,000	$2,610	$2,935	$3,290
Hong Kong	$2,000	$2,610	$2,935	$3,290
Shanghai	$2,150	$2,810	$3,610	$3,545
Shenzhen	$2,200	$2,810	$3,135	$3,490
Dalian	$2,525	$3,310	$3,725	$4,175
Foshan	$2,450	$3,060	$3,385	$3,740
Ningbo	$2,300	$2,910	$3,275	$3,670
Qingdao	$2,450	$3,060	$3,385	$3,740
Xiamen	$2,225	$2,910	$3,275	$3,670
Xingang	$2,225	$2,910	$3,275	$3,670
Yantian	$2,000	$2,610	$2,935	$3,290
Zhongshan	$2,400	$3,010	$3,335	$3,690

freight per item is $0.725 per garment. If there are only 2,400 garments in the container, the cost of freight per garment is $1.09.

A carton that contains product is considered to be a ***master carton***. Master cartons can contain additional ***inner cartons***, which, in turn, contain one or more items. For example, an inner carton may contain three of the same item. If there are four inner cartons, each of which contains three items, then the master carton has four inner cartons for a total of twelve units.

EXAMPLE

$$\frac{\$2,610 \text{ freight from Hong Kong to Long Beach}}{3,600 \text{ units}} = \$0.725$$

$$\frac{\$2,610 \text{ freight from Hong Kong to Long Beach}}{2,400 \text{ units}} = \$1.09$$

The most expensive method of shipping is by air. Charges are determined by the weight of the cartons. Usually buyers consider using air shipments only when product is needed quickly to fill an order or if a factory is running late against a deadline.

Table 07.02 shows freight charges from various overseas ports to Long Beach, California, based on a chart provided by a manufacturer for the year 2004. For more current information, visit Maersk's Web site, www.maersk.com; it is a company headquartered in Copenhagen, with a fleet of more than 250 vessels and offices in more than 125 countries. Under Maersk Logistics, you may view sailing schedules and request a quote on shipping merchandise by boat. Additional information is available on freight forwarders, shipping by air freight, and more. Maersk was named "Carrier of the Year" by Target Corporation in 2004. In May 2005, Wal-Mart honored Maersk for the fourth year in a row with the 2004 "Origin Cargo Manager of the Year " awarded.

DUTY AND CATEGORY CLASSIFICATION

Another expense to take into account is duty. As previously discussed in the text, duty is a tax that U.S. Customs imposes on merchandise imported into the United States. As noted in the previous chapter, the Harmonized Tariff Schedule (HTS) is a system used to establish and list duty by classification and fabric. The United States International Trade Commission monitors the HTS. The CD-ROM includes a portion of the Harmonized Tariff Schedule (Supplement 1, Chapter 62). The rate of duty varies based on the country of origin. To determine if a particular item is duty-free or if a duty rate applies, conduct a search on the U.S. International Trade Commission Interactive Tariff and Trade Data Web site at http://dataweb.usitc.gov.

The category classification for denim trousers is the same three-digit code for women's, girls', men's, and boys'. The ten-digit HTS code provides further detail as to the target user, apparel item, and fabric content. The duty rate for denim trousers is an ad valorem rate, which is the most customary duty rate: it is a percentage of the value of merchandise. If the ad valorem rate is 16.6 percent of the value of the denim trouser and the denim trouser is valued at $10.00, then the duty tax would be $1.66. Two additional types of duty are specific rate and combination rate. Specific rate is based on the weight or quantity of the item to be imported. For example, an imported item purchased in dozens may have a specific rate of $.50 per item. Combination rate is a combination of both ad valorem and specific rates. An example of duty calculation in this situation would be a combination of a percentage of the dollar value of the item plus a specified dollar amount based on weight.

For information regarding classification quota by country, log onto the Web site www.customs.gov and click on textiles and quotas on the left side of the screen. If the quota is absolute, once the allotted amount of goods has entered the United States, no additional goods may enter under that category until quota opens up at the beginning of the following year. If goods have been produced, there will be the expense of warehousing merchandise until quota opens up. If the quota is tariff-rate, a set quantity is permitted to enter the United States at one duty rate. Once the set amount of units has been surpassed, the tariff duty rate increases. Many food products fall under the tariff-rate quota. The Department of Agriculture also controls specific tariff-rate quotas, which require the importer to acquire import licenses. Those who attempt to import products without licenses pay higher duty rates than importers with import licenses.

On January 1, 2004, quotas for products imported into the United States were eliminated for any member of the World Trade Organization (WTO). The exception was textiles and apparel imported from China. "Safeguards" have been placed on certain imports from China as stated in the U.S.–China Memorandum of Understanding (MOU), signed and dated on November 8, 2005. The 18-page memorandum is available on the Customs web site at www.cbp.gov. It is in effect from January 1, 2006 through December 13, 2008.

QUOTATIONS

When the buyer approves the final sample, the factory revises the cost sheet to provide a price quote to the buyer. Figure 07.01 is an example of a completed factory cost sheet for a pair of women's basic six-pocket denim jeans.

The quotation from the supplier to the buyer will include the following information:

* Item number

* Total quantity of units

* Item description and specifications

* Unit type (each, dozen, set)

* FOB (Free on Board) price

* Case dimensions and cubic feet measurement

* Item weight

PERRY'S

Style #: 9203   **Date:** 2/01/06

Description: Boot Cut 6 pocket jean   **Season:** F06

Fabric: 12 oz. Gray cast indigo crosshatch broken twill denim

Sketch

Size	6	8	10	12	14	16
Size Scale	1	2	3	3	2	1

Material	Yardage	Price	Cost
Denim 58" wide	1.5	2.20	$3.30
Total Material			$3.30

Trim/Findings	Quantity	Price	Cost
Zipper 4"	1	.25	$.25
Logo Button 24L	1	.05	.05
Thread	1	.15	.15
Rivets	10	.03	.30
Main Label	1	.05	.05
Care Label	1	.02	.02
Hang tag/price tkt	1	.04	.04
Packaging	1	.15	.15
Total Trim			$1.01

Labor	Cost
Cutting/Sewing	$1.50
Enzyme Wash	$1.00
Total Labor	$2.50

	Description	Cost
Shipping	$8.00 per dozen	$.67
Duty	16.6% of labor/material	$1.13
Overhead	18% of cost	$1.23

Total Manufacturing Cost: $9.84

Markup: 60.6%

Retail Price: $25.00

FIGURE 07.01   *Sample Perry's cost sheet*

- * Gross weight

- * Net weight

- * FOB port

- * Country of origin

- * Minimum order quantity (MOQ)

- * Quantity to fill container

- * Production time

After receiving and accepting the price quote, the buyer writes the order and forwards a quotation form to the manufacturer. Once the manufacturer has received the order, he or she gives an estimate of the delivery date to the buyer. Figure 07.02 is an example of a quotation form.

The FOB price quoted to the buyer is usually the amount it costs to deliver the item to the foreign port of export. It is considered a direct import if the buyer takes possession of the merchandise at the foreign port. The buyer would be responsible for the duty and freight charges from the foreign port of export to the designated U.S. port of entry. If the buyer's company does not work with an overseas freight forwarder, the buyer may request to quote the merchandise at POE cost. This means the buyer will take possession of the merchandise at the U.S. port of entry. The vendor would then quote the POE cost to include the ocean freight and duty. If the buyer is working with a vendor who also operates in the United States and ships merchandise to a warehouse located in the United States, then the buyer could request what is known as an ***indirect import order***. Often when the imported merchandise meets the minimum order quantity but does not fill a container, the supplier ships the merchandise to the U.S. warehouse in a container with other merchandise. In this case, the cost quoted from the supplier includes duty charges, freight from the port of export to the port of entry, and freight from the United States port of entry to the vendor's warehouse. A quote with FOB cost, duty charges, and freight to the port of entry is called the ***estimated laned cost (ELC)***. The merchandise would be ***cross-docked*** at the port of entry. Cross-docked merchandise comes into the warehouse and is turned around and shipped back out to the customer. Since all processing is handled overseas, there is no need to open boxes. Since no domestic warehouse labor is involved, the vendor is able to offer a cost savings to the buyer by giving an additional discount on the wholesale list price.

ABC ENTERPRISES

QUOTATION FORM

COMPANY: ABC Enterprises

CONTACT:

CUSTOMER NAME: Perry's Department Store

DATE: 2/01/06

1	2	3	4	5	6	7	8	9	10	11	12	13	14	15	16	17			18	19	20
Item #	UPC #	Description	Inner	Master	U.M.	Cube	Min. Order Quantity	FOB Cost	Duty %	Duty $	Freight $	Landed cost	Domestic Price	Margin	HTS Code	Case Dimensions LxWxH (inch)			G.W. (lbs)	FOB Port	Vendor
9203		"Boot cut 6-pocket jean, gray"	12	48	ea	1.75	1,200	8.04	16.6	1.33	0.67	10.04	$25.00	59.8	6204624010	36	14	6	24	Shenzhen	ABC

FIGURE 07.02 *Sample quotation form*

ABC ENTERPRISES

ROOM 1033 STAR HOUSE

SALISBURY ROAD

KOWLOON, HONG KONG

TEL: 852 2733 6339

E-MAIL: CWP@ABCENTER.COM

BANKERS:

AGRICULTURAL BANK OF CHINA

23 F. TOWER I, ADMIRALTY CENTRE

18 HARCOURT ROAD

HONG KONG

BUYER:

Perry's Department Store
15203 King Street
Fredericksburg, VA 22401
USA

PRO FORMA NO.: 650

ORDER NO.: PDS01-06

PAYMENT MODE: LC

TERMS: FOB

DATE: 1/02/06

DATE: 1/02/06

PORT: Hong Kong

REF. NO.	DESCRIPTION	PACKING	QUANTITY	PORT	SHIP DATE	RATE US $	AMOUNT
9203	Boot cut 6-pkt jean	12/24	2,400 Ea	Hong Kong		8.04	19,296.00

TOTAL CBM: 87.5

TOTAL FOB US $: 19,296.00

FIGURE 07.03   *Sample pro forma invoice*

PAYMENT FOR THE IMPORTED MERCHANDISE

Sometimes, after receiving a quote, the buyer will request a *pro forma invoice* from the exporter. A pro forma invoice sent at the beginning of a sale includes all information for the sale of the goods as documentation for the buyer to confirm the total cost for the goods. A final invoice will follow when the merchandise is shipped. Figure 07.03 is an example of a pro forma invoice.

Payment for imported merchandise is most often made by *letter of credit*. The company the buyer represents applies to its local bank requesting the letter of credit made payable to the exporter. A letter of credit is a guarantee to the seller that the buyer has the funds to make the purchase, that funds are reserved for the seller, and that payment will be received. Generally, the seller will first send a list of instructions to the buyer for payment by letter of credit, providing details of the bank used by the exporter, where to send the payment, and the specific terms and conditions of the sale. The buyer's bank, known as the issuing bank, notifies the exporter when the letter of credit has been opened and informs the seller of the documents necessary for receipt to release payment. The letter of credit is assigned an expiration date. If the merchandise is not shipped on time, and the transaction will take place after the letter of credit expiration date, the letter of credit must be amended to reflect the new date. Figure 07.04 is an example of a letter of credit.

Another method of payment is by *wire transfer*. The buyer's bank electronically sends money to the seller's bank. While wire transfer is a speedy way to transfer funds, a downside of this method is the seller may want the money before the merchandise is shipped, leaving the buyer with very little control over the merchandise.

The seller may also demand payment by *cash in advance (CIA)*, especially if the buyer is dealing with the exporter for the first time and is not familiar with the buyer's company or if the merchandise is a custom order produced specifically for the buyer. The cash advance is usually required before the seller will ship the goods to the buyer. Sometimes the buyer can negotiate paying a portion, such as one-third of the total cost, in advance of the shipment, with the remaining two-thirds to be payable upon shipment of the goods.

If the buyer needs to finance the import sale, some foreign countries offer financial assistance. Check with the government of the exporting country to see if a financing program is available.

Now that you have selected a country to source denim jeans, examined the laws and requirements pertaining to your product, and verified the classification number and HTS code, you are ready to prepare a cost sheet, quotation form, and

Fredericksburg County Bank

14300 KING STREET
FREDERICKSBURG, VA 22401

DATE OF ISSUE:
2/1/2006 USA

DATE OF EXPIRY:
6/1/2006 USA

IRREVOCABLE DOC. NO.: PDS 4235

APPLICANT:
Perry's Department Store
15203 King Street
Fredericksburg, VA 22401
USA

BENEFICIARY:
ABC Enterprises
Room 1033 Star House
Salisbury Road
Kowloon, Hong Kong

ADVISING BANK:

CURRENCY AMOUNT: USD $19,296.00
U.S. Dollars Nineteen thousand two-hundred ninety-six

Documents to be presented to the negotiating bank within 21 days after date of shipment.

SHIPMENT FROM: Port of Hong Kong
            TO: Port of Norfolk-Newport News, Virginia

TRANSHIPMENT: Not Allowed
PARTIAL SHIPMENT: Not allowed
We hereby issue this irrevocable letter of credit available by negotiation of your draft at sight drawn on the Fredericksburg County Bank, 14300 King Street, Fredericksburg, Virginia, bearing the clause: Drawn under documentary credit number: PDS 4235, for full invoice value of goods accompanied by the following documents:

Invoices, prepared in duplicate
Shipping agent's certificate verifying the vessel adheres to HTS classification
Bill of lading in the name of the Fredericksburg County Bank

MERCHANDISE:
Boot cut 6-pocket jean
AS PER PRO FORMA INVOICE NO.: 650

For the Fredericksburg County Bank	Advising Bank's notification
Authorized signature	place, date, name, and signature of the advising bank

FIGURE 07.04   *Sample letter of credit*

pro forma invoice. After you complete these forms, it is time to contact a bank for a letter of credit.

Using the blank cost sheet in Figure 07.05, fill in the information requested. If you have recently completed a cost sheet from *Perry's Department Store: A Product Development Simulation,* you may use it. If not, choose a pair of denim jeans that you or a friend own, and use them as a guideline along with the example in Figure 07.01 to fill in the blanks.

Next, using the blank quotation form Figure 07.06, fill in information requested. Use the sample quotation form in Figure 07.02 as a guideline, as well as the information from your cost sheet in Figure 07.05.

After you complete the quotation form, complete a pro forma invoice for your denim jeans using the blank form in Figure 07.07. Again, information from your cost sheet and quotation form will provide the necessary facts.

SIMULATION: *Go to Figure 07.05 in the book or CD-ROM.*

SIMULATION: *Go to Figure 07.06 in the book or CD-ROM.*

SIMULATION: *Go to Figure 07.07 in the book or CD-ROM.*

Style #:   **Date:**

Description: **Season:**

Fabric:

Size						
Size Scale						

Material	Yardage	Price	Cost
Total Material			

Trim/Findings	Quantity	Price	Cost
Total Trim			

Labor	Cost
Total Labor	

	Description	Cost
Shipping		
Duty		
Overhead		

Total Manufacturing Cost:

Markup:

Retail Price:

Sketch

FIGURE 07.05   *Perry's cost sheet*

ABC ENTERPRISES

QUOTATION FORM

COMPANY: ABC Enterprises

CONTACT:

CUSTOMER NAME: Perry's Department Store

DATE:

1	2	3	4	5	6	7	8	9	10	11	12	13	14	15	16	17	18	19	20
Item #	UPC #	Description	Inner	Master	U.M.	Cube	Min. Order Quantity	FOB Cost	Duty %	Duty $	Freight $	Landed cost	Domestic Price	Margin	HTS Code	Case Dimensions LxWxH (inch)	G.W. (lbs)	FOB Port	Vendor

FIGURE 07.06   Quotation form

ABC ENTERPRISES

ROOM 1033 STAR HOUSE

SALISBURY ROAD

KOWLOON, HONG KONG

TEL: 852 2733 6339

EMAIL: CWP@ABCENTER.COM

BANKERS:

BUYER:
Perry's Department Store
15203 King Street
Fredericksburg, VA 22401
USA

PROFORMA NO.:

ORDER NO.:

PAYMENT MODE:

TERMS:

DATE:

DATE:

PORT:

REF. NO.	DESCRIPTION	PACKING	QUANTITY	PORT	SHIP DATE	RATE US $	AMOUNT

TOTAL CBM:

TOTAL FOB US $:

FIGURE 07.03 *Sample pro forma invoice*

CHAPTER 8

STEP SEVEN

The Logistics of Importing

Transporting the Import Purchase

IN THIS CHAPTER, YOU WILL LEARN:

* The importance of the Customs-Trade Partnership Against Terrorism
* The types of transportation used when importing textiles and apparel
* What types of boxes are available when packing merchandise
* The type of insurance used to lower the risk of the import

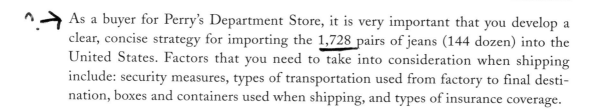

As a buyer for Perry's Department Store, it is very important that you develop a clear, concise strategy for importing the 1,728 pairs of jeans (144 dozen) into the United States. Factors that you need to take into consideration when shipping include: security measures, types of transportation used from factory to final destination, boxes and containers used when shipping, and types of insurance coverage.

SECURITY MEASURES

After the terrorist attack on September 11, 2001, the U. S. Customs and Border Patrol initiated the ***Customs-Trade Partnership Against Terrorism (C-TPAT)***. This is a voluntary partnership agreement among companies involved in the supply chain management of importing products. It is a set of securities measures for all participants whether they are importers, brokers, manufacturers, warehouses, air carriers, sea carriers, land carriers, or air-freight consolidators. By becoming a participant in C-TPAT a company has access to information and can make a decision about whether to do business with a supplier. Figure 08.01 is an abbreviated version of importer instructions for C-TPAT. To see the full list of instructions, go to www.cbp.gov.

C-TPAT PARTNER APPLICATION FOR IMPORTER—INSTRUCTIONS

(Abbreviated version)

IMPORTER FOR C-TPAT
APPLICATION QUALIFICATIONS

1. Active U.S. or Non-Resident Canadian Importer into the United States.

2. Have a business office staffed in the United States or Canada.

3. Have active U.S. importer of record ID(s) in either of the following formats:
   * U.S. Social Security Number
   * U.S. Internal Revenue Service assigned ID(s)
   * CBP assigned Importer ID

4. Possess a valid continuous import bond registered with CBP.

5. Have a designated company officer who will be the primary cargo security officer responsible for C-TPAT.

6. Commit to maintaining CBP C-TPAT supply chain security criteria as outlined in the C-TPAT importer agreement.

7. Create and provide CBP with a C-TPAT supply chain security profile, which identifies how the importer will meet, maintain, and enhance internal policy to meet C-TPAT importer security criteria.

APPLICATION INSTRUCTIONS

Prepare a C-TPAT Supply Chain Security Profile. The security profile should summarize the importer's commitment to ensure adherence to the following C-TPAT security criteria for importers:

SOURCE: U.S. Customs and Border Protection (www.cbp.gov)

FIGURE 08.01: *Supplying the above information to Customs is the first step an importer must take to become a C-TPAT partner. It is worth the effort to become a partner because it helps ensure a more secure and expeditious supply chain.*

SECURITY CRITERIA FOR IMPORTERS

Security measures are in place with all outsources or elements of the supply chain, including, but not limited to, foreign facility, conveyance, or domestic warehouse.

BUSINESS PARTNER REQUIREMENTS

Importers must have written and verifiable processes for the selection of business partners, including manufacturers, product suppliers, and vendors.

SECURITY PROCEDURES

For business partners eligible for C-TPAT certification (carriers, U.S. ports, terminals, brokers, consolidators, etc.) the importer must have documentation (e.g., C-TPAT certificate, SVI number, etc.) indicating whether these business partners are or are not C-TPAT certified.

POINT OF ORIGIN

Importers must ensure business partners develop security processes and procedures consistent with the C-TPAT security criteria to enhance the integrity of shipments at points of origin.

PARTICIPATION /CERTIFICATION IN FOREIGN CUSTOMS ADMINISTRATIONS SUPPLY CHAIN SECURITY PROGRAMS

Current or prospective business partners who have obtained a certification in a supply chain security program being administered by foreign Customs administration should be required to indicate their status of participation to the importer.

CONTAINER INSPECTION

Procedures must be in place to verify the physical integrity of the container structure prior to stuffing, to include the reliability of the locking mechanisms of the doors. A 7-point inspection process is recommended for all containers:

* Front wall
* Left side
* Right side
* Floor
* Ceiling/roof
* Inside/outside doors
* Outside/undercarriage

Most textile and apparel companies are using C-TPAT today; if they are not, then they are in the process of considering security measures for importing products. Typically, the security measures determine if a business is secure so that the risk is reduced. An importer can also avoid conducting business where terrorism is a high-level risk.

LOGISTICS OF TRANSPORTATION

The second consideration in your import strategy is to determine the means of transportation you are going to use. Shipping can add to the cost of the product, which will decrease your profit; therefore, as a buyer, it is important that you understand you can negotiate the price of transportation. The shipping process is a necessary tool in the supply chain. It is also one of the more negotiable items that a buyer can work with to try to get cost down. The following are international terms and their meanings used by buyers and other professionals when shipping product internationally. The list can be found with more in-depth definitions on the web site www.export911.com.

DEPARTURE TERM
EXW Ex works

MAIN CARRIAGE UNPAID
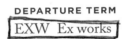
FCA ~~FAC~~ Free carrier
FAS Free alongside ship
FOB Free on Board

MAIN CARRIAGE PAID
CFR Cost and freight
CIF Cost, insurance, and freight
CPT Carriage paid to (location)
CIP Carriage and insurance paid to (location)

ARRIVAL
DAF Delivered at frontier
DES Delivered ex ship
DEQ Delivered ex quay
DDU Delivered duty unpaid
DDP Delivered duty paid

FIGURE 08.02 (LEFT): *This ad from MOL shipping company shows what can happen in the fashion industry if product does not arrive on time.*
SOURCE: MOL (America) Inc.

FIGURE 08.03 (RIGHT): *A vessel shipping containers.*
SOURCE: Photo courtesy of Virginia Port Authority.

Importers may use several means of transportation to get their product from the factory to the final destination. No matter what means of transportation they select to ship their products, it is important that products arrive on time. The ad from MOL—an ocean transportation company, in Figure 08.02—is a very good example of what can happen if a product does not arrive on time.

Shipping from Point A to Point B

There are three basic ways to ship from one country to another: by truck and railway, airway, and ocean freight (Figure 08.03).

Ground transportation is used once the product has entered the port and has been unloaded from the ocean liner or airplane in the form of railroad or truck. Figure 08.04 is a picture of a container handler used to move containers around the shipyard once they are unloaded from the ships. Usually the container is lifted directly from the ship and loaded unto the railcar or truck. Freight forwarders are sometimes used to help with the logistics of moving the goods; they generally receive 2 to 5 percent commission.

FIGURE 08.04 (LEFT): *A straddle carrier at the Port of Virginia moving containers around the shipyard*
SOURCE: Photo courtesy of Virginia Port Authority.

FIGURE 08.05 (RIGHT): *This shipment of containers is entering the Port of Virginia. It is a typical example of how apparel is shipped from a foreign country to the United States.*
SOURCE: Photo courtesy of Virginia Port Authority.

Two basic options to transport textiles and apparel are air freight and ocean freight. Air freight is mostly used by companies that want to be the first to market new trends or want to avoid chargebacks because the merchandise may not reach the destination on time. Air freight is usually not a first option for importers, although it is used by some companies such as high-end retailers or companies that have high profit margins and are able to afford it.

Typically, it is less expensive to use ocean freight, making it the more desirable choice for textile and apparel importers. If an importer uses ocean freight the product will be loaded from the factory. The goods then travel to the port either onto an inland freight carrier or, if the factory is located near the port, directly onto the international freight carrier.

Even before the jeans are transported, they have to be labeled, packaged, and packed. Labeling and packaging of the jeans will be discussed in chapter 9. When

FIGURE 08.06:

These containers are stacked at the Port of Beilun, Ningbo, China. The importer most probably purchased insurance to cover the merchandise inside the containers.

SOURCE: Photo courtesy of Ningbo Economic Trade Development (NETD), Ningbo, China.

packing the jeans, the importer can choose the type of box to use. The next step is to determine the number of boxes to be used for packing the product.

If shipping by air, garment hangers are used and boxing the merchandise is not necessary. With ocean freight, the boxes must be loaded into a container (Figure 08.05). The container is usually leased by the amount of space needed in the shipment. Sometimes it may be a full container or a partial container.

Different containers are used for air than for ocean. Usually an importer will buy space from a ***freight consolidator***, a company that or individual who sells space in a container commonly referred to as less-than-container load (LCL). The freight consolidator will then combine several shipments to fill a container.

LOWERING RISK THROUGH INSURANCE

Conducting business internationally can have certain risks. Lowering the risk by purchasing insurance coverage can help an importer bear the burden should anything occur to the merchandise while in port or en route (Figure 08.06). The basic coverage used once the merchandise leaves the manufacturing plant is known as cargo insurance. The more popular term is marine and inland marine insurance. The marine insurance protects the merchandise while it is in port or being shipped, while inland marine insurance protects the merchandise at other times during shipment whether it is on a truck, an airline, or any other means of transportation used to get the merchandise to the final destination.

An importer can choose to maintain an open insurance policy whereby all shipments are covered over a period of time or a specific policy that is usually only for one shipment. Factors that affect the price of insurance are the value of the merchandise, length of voyage, size of the shipment, reputation of the shipping company, and the packaging of the merchandise. An all-inclusive cargo insurance policy would cover physical loss due to fire, hazardous weather, theft, and pilferage. Insurance coverage does not include loss due to political instability and war.

SIMULATION:

Go to the shipping routes worksheet on the CD-ROM.

As a buyer, you need to determine the cost associated with importing the jeans. Also, you have to decide which modes of transportation will be used and how long it will take from manufacturer to the final designation, which is the distribution center located in Fredericksburg, Virginia. The Web sites for Export 911 (www.export911.com) and the A.P. Moller-Maersk Group (www.maersk.com) are good places to begin your research.

PART I. Determine the following to ship your jeans by ocean freight:

A. Type of box used for packing
B. Number of boxes needed
C. Type of container to be used
D. Space needed in the container based on CBM
E. Create a flow sheet showing means of transportation used
F. Cost to ship jeans
G. Create a timeline from manufacturer to distribution center

PART II. Determine the following to ship your jeans by air freight:

A. Type of garment carrier to be used for packing
B. Number of garment carriers needed
C. Space needed in air freight
D. Create a flow chart showing means of transportation used
E. Cost to ship jeans
F. Create a timeline from manufacturer to distribution center

PART III. Write a synthesis comparing and contrasting the two methods of shipping discussing the advantages and disadvantages of each.

CHAPTER 9

STEP EIGHT

The Entry Process

Importing Processes and Procedures for Textiles and Apparel

IN THIS CHAPTER, YOU WILL LEARN:

* The organization of the U.S. Customs and Border Protection Department
* The importing procedure associated with textiles and apparel
* What basic documents are used in the importing process
* The facilitation of the entry process used by U.S. Customs and Border Protection Department

This chapter focuses on the role that U.S. Customs plays in the importation of denim jeans. You will learn about the organization of the U.S. Customs and Border Protection Department, importing procedure, documents used in importing, and importing entry process.

The U.S. Customs agency has the responsibility of enforcing some 400 laws and regulations on international traffic and trade. Its responsibilities include controlling and facilitating the movement of carriers, people, and commodities between the United States and countries around the world; protecting domestic industry against unfair foreign competition; investigating the smuggling of illegal goods in and out of the country; and investigating the activities intended to avoid payment of duties and taxes.

There are 20 Customs Management Centers (CMC) located throughout the United States. A CMC director followed by service and area port directors and port directors head each center. The import transactions are implemented at service ports, area ports, and ports of entry. There are U.S. Customs offices located throughout the world to help the U.S. importer receive their commodities from foreign exporters.

The importing process is not easy, but all importers must comply with the rules, regulations, and laws associated with importing textiles and apparel. Refer to the U.S.

INVOICE

Chang Denim Co., Ltd.

CHANGXING INDUSTRIAL PARK,
JUN'AN TOWN, SHUNDE DISTRICT,
FOSHAN CITY, GUANGDONG PROVINCE, CHINA   528329
TELEPHONE: 84-747-25277777, 24482555

ACCOUNT:

Perry's Department Store
15203 King Street
Fredericksburg, VA 22401
USA

SHIPMENT FROM: Guangdong Province, China to Fredericksburg, VA

SHIPMENT VIA: Maersk Shipping

COUNTRY OF ORIGIN: China

STYLE #	DESCRIPTION	P.O. #	QUANTITY	UNIT PRICE	TOTAL PRICE
1849	Ladies' denim jeans	103459	1,728	11.90/ea.	$20,563.20
			1,728		$20,563.20

Chang Denim Company

FIGURE 09.01   *Sample invoice from manufacturer*

Customs and Border Protection Department Web site at http://www. cbp.gov for publications about informed compliance in the "What Every Member of the Trade Community Should Know About..." series. These publications answer any additional questions you may have about the regulations and laws associated with importing.

THE IMPORT PROCEDURE

At the beginning of the importing simulation you ordered 1,728 pairs of jeans from a manufacturer in your assigned country. When you placed your order, it was considered a sales contract, which is in the form of a purchase order. A purchase order is a legally binding contract stating that you have ordered the jeans and agree to pay a certain amount once you are billed in the form of an invoice (Figure 09.01). You agree to pay and choose the method of payment: either a letter of credit, the most common method of payment, or a draft issued by a commercial bank with which you conduct business. Your bank asks the corresponding bank in the country from which you are exporting to confirm the amount and terms of the letter of credit. Once both banks and the importer and manufacturer agree on the terms, the manufacturer prepares the goods and other documentation for importing.

DOCUMENTS AND FORMS USED IN THE IMPORT PROCEDURE

Documents and forms are used in the import procedure to make sure all information is recorded and in a format acceptable by U.S. Customs. The documents used for importing textiles and apparel typically fall into four major categories: banking, transportation, commercial, and government. Banking documents are required for the seller to get paid. As you learned earlier, the letter of credit is the most common form of payment. Other forms of payment include advanced payments, bank drafts, or, if there is an ongoing relationship between the importer and manufacturer, with an open account. Transportation documents deal with the logistics of moving the product and include a packing list, bills of lading, insurance certificate, and arrival notice and delivery orders. Government documents include certificate of origin, entry summaries, and the shippers import declaration and can be found on the U.S. Customs' Web site. Commercial documents are generated by the seller and include a commercial invoice, pro forma invoice, and insurance certificate. Refer to Table 09.01 for a complete explanation of each of the documents.

FORMS AND DOCUMENTS ASSOCIATED WITH IMPORTING JEANS

NAME	PURPOSE
FORMS/DOCUMENTS GENERATED BY THE BUYER (IMPORTER)	
Power of Attorney	A written document authorizing a person (usually a U.S. Customs agent), to act as an agent for another person (importer), as noted on the document.
Entry Summary	Filed within 10 days of the shipment being released, with estimated duties deposited within 10 working days.
GSP Form	Serves as a certificate of origin of product. Sometimes referred to as the certificate of origin.
FORMS/DOCUMENTS GENERATED BY FREIGHT CARRIERS	
Ocean Bill of Lading	A receipt for the cargo and a contract for transportation between a shipper and the ocean carrier.
Inland Bill of Lading	An inland bill of lading is used as the transportation of the goods between the port, factory, and the point of destination. Information included on the bill of lading includes marks, numbers, steamship line, and similar information that matches with a dock receipt.
Insurance Certificate	Formal document showing the value of the goods insured for the value of the cargo, taxes, and duties.
Arrival Notice	Sent by the freight company to the importer to notify about the arrival of goods.
Intermodal Bill of Lading	Can be used if more than one mode of transportation is being used to transport goods.
FORMS/DOCUMENTS GENERATED BY THE SELLER (MANUFACTURER)	
Packing List	Similar to a commercial invoice, one copy is attached to the box for U.S. Customs to use as a checklist for the incoming product; another copy is inside the box. Financial information is not included on a packing list.
Commercial Invoice	In accordance with the Tariff Act, this document must include the port of entry, name of buyer and seller, name of shipper and receiver, description of merchandise, quantity of each product being shipped, purchase price, number of packages being shipped, and the country of origin.
Pro Forma Invoice	May be issued prior to shipping textiles and apparel. The seller sends this invoice with the terms of sale and description of product. Generally used if the required commercial invoice has not been filed at the time the merchandise enters the United States.
FORMS/DOCUMENTS GENERATED BY BANK	
Letter of Credit	A letter of credit is a document issued by a bank stating its commitment to pay someone (supplier/exporter/seller) a stated amount of money on behalf of a buyer (importer) so long as the seller meets very specific terms and conditions. The terms and conditions listed in the credit all involve presenting specific documents within a certain period of time.
Insurance Certificate	Document stating that the goods being imported are covered by certain risks and presigned by the insurer.

Once the shipment reaches the United States, the importer files all entry documents with the port director at the port of entry. Three things have to take place for goods to legally enter into the United States: (1) shipment must arrive at the designated port of entry, (2) delivery of merchandise must be authorized by U.S. Customs, and (3) estimated duties must be paid.

Now your jeans are at the port and the entry must take place, which is commonly referred to as "clearing customs." The following section focuses on the steps Customs goes through prior to releasing the jeans.

THE ENTRY PROCESS

You have just learned about the documents associated with importing. Now you will learn what to do with the completed documents. The entry is made by the owner of the goods or whoever has been designated power of attorney. The entry process has five basic steps: entry, examination and inspection, valuation, classification, and liquidation.

Entry

Once the goods have arrived, the importer or the person acting on his or her behalf (such as a customs broker) has five days to file an entry package. Most, if not all, of the process is paperless, and is handled electronically with software such as Automated Broker Interface (ABI). Entry documents include entry manifest, evidence of right to make entry, commercial or pro forma invoice, packing lists, and a surety bond.

Examination and Inspection

Prior to release of the goods, the port director will designate representative quantities of the shipment to be examined. There is someone at the port who inspects the merchandise to determine that the goods are marked properly, correctly invoiced, not in excess or short of the invoiced quantities, and contain no prohibited articles.

Valuation

Valuation refers to the transaction value of merchandise imported into the United States. It is the price actually paid (or payable) for the merchandise plus amounts for the packing costs, selling commission, value of any **assist**, and any royalty or license fee. If it is not possible to determine the value by appraising identical or similar merchandise, Customs will make its own appraisal based on the cost listed on the invoice.

Classification

Most textiles and apparel imported into the United States are subject to duty. As you learned earlier in the text, if merchandise is not duty-free, ad valorem, specific, or combined rates will be assessed. Rates of duty vary, depending on the country of origin for the merchandise.

Liquidation

This is the final step in the entry process. Usually a Customs official reviews the entry and determines whether proper duty has been paid. Once this occurs the importer receives notice that liquidation has taken pace. Normally, you will receive your goods before the final step, since you have filed an insurance certificate, Customs is assured that duty will be paid. If you disagree with the amount of duty charged by Customs, you may file a protest within 90 days from the date of liquidation. This can be for an adjustment in the rate of duty or a refund. If the protest is denied, an importer has 180 days to file a summons with the U.S. Court of International Trade. Liquidation is not final until all litigation has been resolved.

SIMULATION:
Go to the entry process worksheet on the CD-ROM.

Create an entry package using the forms and documents associated with importing jeans. Write a two-page paper discussing the process and defining the forms and documents used. You can begin your research with the U.S. Customs and Border Control (www.cbp.gov) and Export 911 (www.export911.com) Web sites.

CHAPTER 10

Career Opportunities in Importing

IN THIS CHAPTER, YOU WILL LEARN:

* The diverse careers available in the area of importing
* The various businesses involved in importing
* The roles, skills, and responsibilities that occupations in importing involve

This chapter provides insight into employment opportunities for importing merchandise from foreign countries into the United States. The focus is on careers in retail companies, merchandise buying offices, the U.S. Office of Customs and Border Protection, and manufacturers based in the United States who import merchandise. It will also discuss the job of a sales agent who handles importing product and the job of a Customs broker. There is a listing of various positions along with job descriptions and skill requirements. This is a helpful section for students who are interested in the field of importing.

RETAIL BUYER, ASSOCIATE BUYER, SENIOR ASSISTANT BUYER

Many retail operations are large enough to support the minimum quantity required to purchase imported merchandise. This includes department stores, chain stores, large specialty store operations, and some catalog companies, just to name a few. Generally, retail buyers are responsible for import purchases of selected categories in their department. Buyers may purchase imported merchandise from buying offices with which their companies are associated, through manufacturers based in the United States, by means of sales agents, or directly from factories located overseas. Buyers may also use the services of Customs brokers.

If a buyer is purchasing through a buying office, the buyer may travel to the office to attend import meetings approximately twice a year, once for spring and summer purchases and again for fall and winter purchases. The schedule depends on the type of product to be purchased. Import purchases may be planned six months to a year in advance of the desired shipping period. When buying through a buying office, there is the benefit of combining quantity with other store members for advantageous volume pricing. Some buyers will accompany the buying office merchandising representative on the trip overseas to work with the factory to develop product. The buying office representative is responsible for following up on production of merchandise selected by the buyer for import.

Buyers may also work with vendors based in the United States who offer direct importing of merchandise to stores that have the ability to purchase container loads of product. Buyers may select from in-line product or may develop exclusive goods customized to their needs. Manufacturers are responsible for overseeing production and ensuring quality of merchandise with their overseas factories.

A buyer who does not belong to a buying office may choose to go through an agent to purchase import merchandise. The agent assists the buyer in sourcing factories to produce merchandise and acts as a liaison for all transactions of the process. The agent communicates with the factory to make certain the goods are produced to specification.

A buyer may also have a professional relationship with a company overseas and visit the factory directly to develop and produce merchandise for import. In this case, the buyer is responsible for all communication with the factory.

Retail buyers are generally required to have a college education. To be promoted to the level of buyer, experience as an assistant buyer, and possibly experience in a sales management position, may be required. The level above an assistant buyer at larger stores is associate buyer. Associate buyers and senior assistant buyers may be given categories to buy under the direction of senior buyers. Associate buyers may be in charge of importing merchandise in their categories of responsibility. Other retail management positions above the level of buyer are also involved in the purchase of imported merchandise.

Importing product is just one aspect of the buyer's responsibility. The buyer's main role is to plan, manage, and attain the financial goal for the department or departments in which he or she works. The buyer is responsible for achieving planned sales, markdowns, gross margin, and turnover. The buyer negotiates with vendors to select and monitor an assortment of appropriate domestic or imported merchandise for his or her area of responsibility.

Qualifications

To become a retail buyer, two or more years of experience in the buying office as an assistant or associate buyer is required. The amount of experience depends on the size of the retail operation and the number of departments assigned to the buyer. Buyers must be proficient in strategic planning and forecasting, possess strong analytical ability, and exhibit excellent oral and written communication skills. It is necessary to be detail-oriented, have a sense of urgency, and be able to handle multiple tasks.

The positions of associate buyer and senior assistant buyer generally require at least 18 months experience as assistant buyers. The same basic skills listed for a buyer are essential for the associate or senior assistant. At this level, they should be familiar with retail math formulas and demonstrate strong computer skills, with knowledge of Excel.

DIVISIONAL MERCHANDISE MANAGER

Buyers report to a divisional merchandise manager (DMM). The DMM is typically in charge of several similar departments of merchandise. The DMM is responsible for leading the strategic planning and meeting the financial goals of his or her division. The DMM guides buyers within the division on import planning and purchases. The DMM may also accompany the buyer on overseas trips or go in place of the buyer.

Qualifications

Promotion to the level of DMM requires at least four years of experience in buying and store management. In addition to the qualifications of a buyer, a DMM must demonstrate strong leadership skills. It is the role of the DMM to develop the division team.

GENERAL MERCHANDISE MANAGER

A general merchandise manager (GMM) is one level above the DMM. In most retail stores, there is a GMM for soft goods, including apparel, cosmetics, and accessories, and a GMM for hard lines, including housewares, tabletop, electronics and small appliances, gifts, domestics, and so on. The role of the GMM is much the same as the DMM, except that the GMM is responsible for more than one division.

Qualifications

Experience in buying, store management, and at least two years in the role of DMM are needed for the position of GMM.

DIRECTOR OF IMPORTS

Some retail operations also have an import director who is responsible for overseeing all departments and importing product for the store. The import director assists buyers in planning import purchases and travels overseas with buyers to attend trade shows and appointments with vendors. If the retail operation uses an agent overseas to procure merchandise for import, the import director is the liaison.

Qualifications

The qualifications of a director of imports are the same as a DMM's. An import director would more than likely have been a DMM, with many years of importing experience.

The sections above offer a basic overview of positions in a retail store buying division. Job titles and descriptions vary depending on the size and breadth of each retail company. Most major retailers have Web sites listing career opportunities. In the search window of your Internet provider, type in the name of the store that interests you to locate the Web site and research available positions. Along with a job description, most companies list detailed qualifications for the position.

MERCHANDISING GROUPS AND BUYING OFFICE POSITIONS

Merchandising group or buying office positions are similar to those of the retail store buyer. Responsibilities include shopping the market, both domestically and overseas, to recommend merchandise assortments suitable for their member stores or clients and to develop private label merchandise for exclusivity and value. In addition to seeking new trends, merchandising groups and buying offices often look to retail store buyers to report best-selling merchandise to source overseas at reduced prices and maximize sales. They also scout the overseas markets for merchandise unique to the particular country of sourcing. Some buying office representatives travel overseas with a team of key buyers from member stores. A buying office may have DMM and GMM positions, as do retail operations. In this case, roles follow the pattern of the retail store.

Qualifications

The qualifications of a market representative, DMM, and GMM reflect the characteristics required of the comparable retail ranks of retail buyer, DMM, and GMM. All positions demand previous buying experience of both domestic and imported merchandise.

The three leading merchandise groups are Macy's Merchandise Group of Federated Department Stores, Associated Merchandising Corporation (AMC) owned by Target Corporation, and Saks Department Store Group. May Merchandising Group of May Department Stores Company was formerly a leading buying group that announced a merger with Federated Department Stores in 2005. AMC and Macy's Merchandise Group have additional career opportunities.

AMC offers career paths in global sourcing, business management, production, global operations, and other technical areas. Macy's Merchandising Group has a Web site dedicated to career choices within Macy's and Federated's various divisions at www.retailology.com. There are buttons to click to search for jobs and for information on college recruitment. Look for jobs in locations throughout the United States at Macy's retail divisions, the home office in New York, and Federated headquarters in Cincinnati, Ohio. Career paths for Saks Department Store Group can be found on the Web site at www.saksincorporated.com.

AGENT

Buyers who are unfamiliar with factories and language overseas may enlist the services of an *agent*. The role of the agent is to determine the needs of the buyer and direct the buyer to appropriate sources. The agent negotiates the terms of purchase for the buyer and guides the buyer in proper importing procedures. An agent is paid commission based on a percentage of the dollar amount of the total purchase. Agents may have a corporate office with a support staff, or work as an individual out of an office located in the agent's home. Agents often live near a port.

Qualifications

An agent must be fluent in English as well as the language of the country he or she represents. An agent must also be familiar with the market and products available. Good negotiation skills and knowledge of import laws are required. An agent must also possess computer skills, as much of the communication is conducted through e-mail. Agents should be familiar with all procedures of import and export. Additional qualifications vary by country.

CUSTOMS BROKER

A Customs broker assists importers and exporters in transporting merchandise through U.S. Customs. A broker completes the necessary paperwork for entry and classification, as well as advises the importer of duties and fees owed to Customs. The broker may deliver payment on behalf of the buyer and arrange for delivery of the merchandise to the importer. Brokers may work for a brokerage firm or independently. Brokers generally live in close proximity to a port.

The best Web site to view is the U.S. Customs and Border Protection's at www.customs.gov/xp/cgov/import. The definition of a Customs broker and requirements for the position are outlined there. Additionally, The National Customs Brokers and Forwarders Association of America, Inc. has a Web site at www.ncbfaa.org.

Qualifications

A Customs broker may work for a small or large agency or independently. In the United States, a Customs broker must be at least 21 years of age and licensed by the importer's government. In the United States, brokers must apply for their licenses and take the exam at the port where they will offer services. Customs will conduct a background search on all individuals applying for a Customs broker license. All licensed brokers must file a status report every three years.

UNITED STATES OFFICE OF CUSTOMS AND BORDER PROTECTION

U.S. Customs and Border Protection is responsible for controlling international trade and security at the U.S. ports of entry. This is a U.S. government office under the Department of Homeland Security.

In Customs, an import specialist communicates with importers and exporters to verify classification and valuation of merchandise. It is the job of the import specialist to decide what merchandise can enter the United States, based on U.S. trade laws.

An entry specialist handles paperwork generated from the import specialists. The person in this position also assists importers and brokers with bonds.

More than one specialist works at a Customs office. A team leader heads each team of specialists. For further information on positions within the Office of Customs and Border Protection, visit the Web site at www.CBP.gov. Specific job opportunities are listed at www.usajobs.gov and www.ntis.gov/jobs/jobsearch.aspx.

Qualifications

A college degree is required to obtain a position as a specialist. At the G-5 entrance level of this government occupation, three years of general experience is required in addition to a bachelor's degree. Employees may start at higher levels if they have more years of specialized experience relating to the position desired. A specialist must be highly organized, have keen analytical skills, and must be knowledgeable in import and export trade as well as international trade laws.

PRODUCT DEVELOPMENT, IMPORT MANUFACTURER

A manufacturer who imports merchandise may have an office at an overseas location or contract out to factories to produce goods to import. The manufacturer may use the services of an agent to assist in sourcing factories to produce goods. A line manager or product manager on the product development team of the U.S. manufacturer develops a line two to four times a year, communicating design and specifications of product with the overseas office or agents. They also travel to trade shows, both domestically and overseas, to look for trends and seek unique products, ideas, and sources. European shows are the best for scouting out the latest trends in color and design. Shows in China and India are the best for sourcing factories to produce merchandise at a value price.

Many manufacturers maintain an import department to handle the logistics once the line manager or product manager has developed a product. The import analyst places the order for product development and monitors production and transportation of the merchandise. It is also the duty of the import department to determine the classification, valuation, and duty rates of an item through a Customs office. To find jobs with a manufacturer, the best resource is a trade publication for the industry of interest. The job listing is generally in the back of the publication under classifieds. The following Fairchild trade publications and Web sites cover women's apparel and accessories, men's apparel and furnishings, children's apparel and accessories, and home textiles:

Women's Wear Daily (WWD), www.WWD.com

Daily News Record (DNR), www.DNRNews.com

Children's Business, www.ChildrensBusiness.com

Home Furnishing News, www.HFNMag.com

Qualifications

A college degree is preferred for a position in product development or the import department. The person must demonstrate strong analytical skills and be able to negotiate and handle multiple tasks in a fast-paced environment. Excellent oral and written communication skills are essential. It is helpful, but not necessary, to speak the language of the country of export. For product development, creativity is an essential characteristic.

Helpful Web Site Resources

TRADE PUBLICATIONS AND INFORMATION SOURCES

Apparel (formerly Bobbin): www.apparelmag.com/

Apparel News: www.apparelnews.net

Apparel Search: www.apparelsearch.com

Children's Business: www.childrensbusiness.com

Daily News Record (*DNR*): Men's fashion weekly publication on Monday, www.dailynewsrecord.com

Emerging Textiles: textile and apparel trade info www.emergingtextiles.com

Just-Style: textile, apparel, and footwear industry newsletter www.just-style.com

Textile Industries: www.textileindustries.com

Textile Solutions: textile developments www.TextileSolutions.com

Textile World: www.textileworld.com

Women's Wear Daily (*WWD*): www.wwd.com

AGENCIES, ASSOCIATIONS, AND ORGANIZATIONS

American Apparel and Footwear Association: www.americanapparel.org/

Andean Community (CAN): www.comunidadandina.org

American Association of Exporters and Importers: www.aaci.org

Apparel Net: http://apparelnet.com

Export/import information and INCOTERMS: www.export911.com

Federation of International Trade Associations: www.fita.org

Global Sources, product and trade information: www.globalsources.com

Import Administration, U.S. Department of Commerce: www.ia.ita.doc.gov

International Trade Centre (ITC): www.intracen.org

Office of Textiles and Apparel: www.otexa.ita.doc.gov

Office of the United States Trade Representative: www.ustr.gov

The World Factbook: www.cia.gov/cia/publications/factbook

Tradeport: www.tradeport.org/countries/

United Nations Industrial Development Organization (Unido): www.unido.org

U.S. Association of Importers of Textiles and Apparel: www.usaita.com

United Nations: http://www.un.org

United States Customs and Border Protection: www.cbp.gov

United States Department of Commerce: www.doc.gov

United States Federal Trade Commission: www.ftc.gov

United States International Trade Commission: www.usitc.gov

United States International Trade Commission, Department of Commerce: www.ita.doc.gov

World Trade Organization: www.wto.org

ECONOMIC AND STATISTICAL INFORMATION

Currency Converter: www.xe.com/ucc/
Foreign Trade Statistics: www.census.gov/foreign-trade/www/
International Finance Corporation: http://globaledge.msu.edu
International Monetary Fund: www.imf.org
International Trade Statistics: www.intracen.org/tradstat
Office of Trade and Economic Analysis: www.trade.gov/tradestats
Organization for Economic Cooperation and Development (OECD): www.oecd.com
United States Census Bureau: www.census.gov, www.factfinder.census.gov
United States Statistical Information: www.stat-usa.com
World Bank: www.worldbank.org

COUNTRY PROFILE INFORMATION

Library of Congress: www.memory.loc.gov/frd/cs/cshome.html
International Trade Administration: www.trade.gov/td/tic/
The Office of Textiles and Apparel: www.otexa.ita.doc.gov
U.S. Department of State: www.state.gov

FREDERICKSBURG, VIRGINIA INFORMATION

www.co.caroline.va.us
www.fact-index.com
www.simplyfredericksburg.com
www.fredericksburgvirginia.net
http://fredericksburg.com
www.fredericksburgva.gov

Service Ports and Area Ports

PORT	ADDRESS	PHONE	FAX
Anchorage, AK 99501	605 W. Fourth Avenue	907-271-2675	907-271-2684
Atlanta, GA 30354	700 Doug Davis Drive	404-763-7020	404-763-7038
Baltimore, MD 21202	40 S. Gay Street	410-962-2666	410-962-9335
Baton Rouge, LA 70309	5353 Essen Lane	504-389-0261	504-389-0260
Blaine, WA 98230	9901 Pacific Highway	360-332-5771	360-332-4701
Boston, MA 02222-1059	10 Causeway Street, Suite 603	617-565-6147	617-565-6137
Buffalo, NY 14202	111 W. Huron Street	716-646-3400	716-551-5011
Calais, ME 04619	One Maine Street	207-454-3621	207-454-7122
Calexico, CA 92231	One Maine Street	760-768-2300	760-768-2301
Champlain, NY 12919	198 West Service Road	518-298-8311	518-298-8314
Charleston, SC 29401	200 E. Bay Street	843-579-6500	843-579-6611
Charlotte, NC 28217	1901-K Cross Beam Drive	704-329-6100	704-329-6103
Charlotte/Amalie, VI	Main Post Office Sugar Estate/ St. Thomas Virgin Islands 00801	340-774-2510	340-776-3489
Chicago, IL 60607-4523	610 Canal Street	312-353-6100	312-353-2337
Christiansted, VI	PO Box 249 /St. Croix Virgin Islands 00820	809-773-1490	809-778-7419
Cleveland, OH 44130	6747 Engle Road Middleburg Heights	440-891-3800	440-891-3836
Dallas/Ft. Worth, TX 75261	PO Box 619050 DFW Airport	972-574-2170	972-574-4818
Denver, CO 80239	4735 Oakland Street	303-361-0712	303-361-0722
Derby Line, VT 05830	Interstate 91	802-873-3489	802-873-3628
Detroit, MI 48226	477 Michigan Avenue, Suite 200	313-226-3177	313-226-3179
Douglas, AZ 85607	First Street and Pan American Avenue	520-364-8486	520-364-2313
Duluth, MN 55801	515 W. First Street	218-720-5201	218-720-5216

El Paso, TX 79907	797 S. Zaragosa Road	915-872-5721	915-872-5723
Grand Rapids, MI 49512	Kent County Airport	616-456-2515	616-285-0188
Great Falls, MT 59401	21 Third Street North, Suite 201	406-453-7631	406-453-7069
Greenville/ Spartansburg, SC	150-A West Phillips Road Greer, SC 29650	864-877-8006	864-848-3454
Harrisburg, PA	Harrisburg International Airport, Building #135 Middletown, PA 17057-5035	717-782-4510	717-948-9294
Hartford, CT 06103	135 High Street	860-240-4306	860-240-4309
Highgate Springs, VT	RR2, BOX 170 Swanton, VT 05488	802-240-4306	802-240-2373
Honolulu, HI 96813	101 Bishop Street Pacific Tower 25th Floor	808-522-2778	808-522-8081
Houlton, ME 04730	RR 3, Box 5300	207-532-2131	207-532-6622
Houston/Galveston, TX	2350 N. Sam Houston Parkway E. Suite 1000 Houston, TX 77032	281-985-6700	281-985-6706
Jacksonville, FL 32206	2831 Talleyrand Avenue	904-232-3476	904-232-1992
Kansas City, MO 64116	4100 North Mulberry Drive Room 110	816-584-1994	816-584-8431
Laredo/Colombia, TX	PO Box 3130 Laredo, TX 78044	956-726-2267	956-726-2948
Los Angeles Airport Area, CA	11099 S. La Cienega Boulevard Los Angeles, CA 90045	310-215-2618	310-215-2013
Los Angeles/Long Beach Seaport Area, CA	300 S. Ferry Street Terminal Island, CA 90731	310-514-6003	310-514-6769
Louisville, KY 40202	601 W. Broadway	502-582-5186	502-625-7224
Miami Airport, FL	6601 N.W., 25th Street Miami, FL 33102	305-869-2800	305-869-2822
Miami Seaport, FL	1500 Port Boulevard Miami, FL 33132	305-536-5260	305-536-5282
Milwaukee, WI	6269 Ace Industrial Drive Cudahy, WI 53110	414-571-2860	414-762-0253
Minneapolis, MN 55401	2nd Avenue, South, Suite 560	612-348-1690	612-348-1630
Mobile, AL 36602	150 N. Royal Street, Room 3004	334-441-5106	334-441-6061
Nashville, TN 37227	PO Box 270008	615-736-5861	615-736-5331
New Orleans, LA 70130	423 Canal Street	504-670-2391	504-670-2123
Newark, NJ 07102	1100 Raymond Boulevard	973-368-6100	973-368-6991
New York/JFK Area	Building #77, JFK Jamaica, NY 11430	718-553-1542	718-553-0077
New York/Newark Area	1210 Corbin Street Elizabeth, NJ 07201	201-443-0200	201-443-0550

Nogales, AZ 85261	9 N. Grand Avenue	520-287-1410	520-287-1421
Norfolk, VA 23510	200 Granby Street, Suite 839	757-441-3400	757-441-6630
Ogdensburg, NY 13669	127 N. Water Street	315-393-0660	315-393-7472
Orlando, FL 32827	5390 Bear Road	407-825-4300	407-648-6827
Oroville, WA 98844	Route 1, Box 130	509-476-2955	509-476-2465
Otay Mesa, CA	9777 Via de la Amistad San Diego, CA 92173	619-661-3305	619-661-3049
Pembina, ND 58271	112 W. Stutsman Street	701-825-6201	701-825-6473
Philadelphia, PA 19106	2nd and Chestnut Streets	215-597-4606	215-597-8370
Phoenix, AZ 85034	3002 E. Old Tower Road, Suite 400	602-914-1400	602-914-1409
Port Huron, MI 48060	526 Water Street	810-985-7125	810-985-3516
Portland, ME 04101	312 Fore Street	207-780-3327	207-780-3420
Portland, OR 97238	PO Box 55580	503-326-2865	506-326-3511
Providence, RI 02905	49 Pavilion Avenue	401-941-6326	401-941-6628
Raleigh/Durham, NC	120 Southcenter Court, Suite 500 Morrisville, NC 27560	919-467-3552	919-467-0706
Richmond, VA 23231	4501 Williamsburg Road, Suite G	804-226-9675	804-226-1197
San Antonio, TX 78216	9800 Airport Boulevard	210-821-6965	210-821-6968
San Francisco, CA 94111	555 Battery Street	415-782-9200	415-705-1226
San Juan, PR 00901	Number One La Puntilla Street, Room 214	787-729-6850	787-729-6678
San Luis, AZ 85349	PO Box H	520-627-8854	520-627-9850
San Ysidro, CA 94111	720 E. San Ysidro Boulevard	619-662-7201	619-622-7374
Sault Ste. Marie, MI 49783	International Bridge Plaza	906-632-7221	912-652-4435
Savannah, GA 31401	1 East Bay Street	912-652-4256	912-652-4435
Seattle, WA 98104-1049	1000 2nd Avenue, Suite 2100	206-553-6527	206-553-2940
St. Albans, VT 05478	PO Box 1490	802-524-6527	802-527-1338
St. Louis, MO 63134	4477 Woodson Road	314-428-2662	314-428-289
Syracuse, NY 13212	4034 S. Service Road North	315-455-8446	315-454-8224
Tacoma, WA 98421	2202 Port of Tacoma Road	253-593-6336	253-593-6351
Tampa, FL 33605	1624 E. Seventh Avenue, Suite 101	813-228-2385	813-225-7309
Tuscon, AZ 85706	7150 S. Tuscon Boulevard	520-670-6461	520-670-6648
Washington, D.C. 20041	PO Box 17423	703-318-5900	703-318-6706
Wilmington, NC 28401	One Virginia Ave.	910-815-4601	910-815-4581

SOURCE: U.S. Customs and Border Protection

United States Customs Officers in Foreign Countries

AUSTRIA
Customs Attaché
American Embassy
Boltzmanngasse 16
A-1091 Vienna
Tel: 011-43-1-313-39-2112

BELGIUM
U.S. Mission to the European
Communities
40 Boulevard du Regent
B-1000
Brussels
Tel: 011-322-209-9334

CANADA
Customs Attaché
U.S. Customs Service
490 Sussex Drive
Ottawa, Ontario
K1N 1G8
Tel: 613-238-4470, Ext. 322

CHINA
Customs Attaché
American Embassy
XIV SHUI BEI JIE2
Beijing, 100600
People's Republic of China
Tel: 011-86-10-6500-3012

COLOMBIA
Customs Attaché
American Embassy
Carrera 45 #22D
Santa Fe de Bogota, Colombia
Tel: 011-571-315-2162

FRANCE
Customs Attaché
American Embassy
58 bis Rue la Boetie
75008 Paris
Tel: 331-4312-7400

GERMANY
American Embassy
U.S. Customs Service
Customs Attaché Clayalle 170
14195 Berlin
Tel: 011-49-30-8305-1470

U.S. Customs Service
American Consulate
Platenstrasse 9
60320 Frankfurt AM Main
Tel: 011-49-69-7535-3630

HONG KONG
American Consulate General
11/F., St. John's Building
33 Garden Road
Room 221
Central, Hong Kong
Tel: 011-852-2230-5100

ITALY
Customs Attaché
American Embassy
Via Veneto 119
00187 Rome
Tel: 011-39-06-4674-2475

JAPAN
Customs Attaché
American Embassy
10-5, Alaska 1-Chome
Minato-ku
Tokyo 107-8420
Tel: 011-813-3224-5433

KOREA
Customs Attaché
American Embassy
82 SeJong-Ro
Chongro-Ku
Seoul 110-050
Tel: 011-822-397-4644

MEXICO
Senior Customs Representative
American Consulate General
Monterrey 141 Poniente
Hermosillo, Sonora
Tel: 011-52-6212-3971

Customs Attaché
American Embassy
Paseo de la Reforma 305
Colonia Cuauhtemoc
Mexico City, D.F.
Tel: 011-525-209-9100

Sr. Customs Representative
American Consulate General
Avenida Constitucion
411 Poniente
Monterrey Mexico, N.L. 6430
Tel: 011-528-342-7972

PANAMA

Customs Attaché
American Embassy
Calle 38 y Avenida Balboa
Panama City
Tel: 011-507-225-7562

RUSSIA

Customs Attaché
American Embassy
19-23 Novinsky Boulevard
Moscow 121099
Tel: 011-7-095-728-5050

SINGAPORE

Customs Attaché
American Embassy
27 Napier Road
Singapore 258508
Tel: 011-65-476-9020

SOUTH AFRICA

Customs Attaché
America Embassy
877 Pretorius
Arcadia, Pretoria 0001
Tel: 011-27-12-342-8062

THAILAND

Customs Attaché
Sindhorn Building
130-132 Wireless Road
Tower 2, 12th Floor
Bangkok 10330
Tel: 011-66-2-205-5015

UNITED KINGDOM

Customs Attaché
American Embassy
24/31 Grosvenor Square
London, W1A 1AE
Tel: 011-44-207-409-1293

URUGUAY

Customs Attaché
American Embassy
1776 Lauro Muller Montevideo
Tel: 011-598-2-411-1835

VENEZUELA

Customs Attaché
Calle B con Calle F
Cloinas de Valle Ariba Caracas
Tel: 001-58-212-975-9110

See the U.S. Department of State web site (http://foia.state.gov) for the most updated information.

SOURCE: U.S. Department of State

United States Customs Management Centers

ARIZONA
4740 North Oracle Road
Tuscon, AZ 85705
520-670-5900
Fax 520-670-5911

CARRIBBEAN AREA
#1 La Puntilla Street
San Juan, PR 00901
787-729-6950
Fax 787-729-6978

EAST GREAT LAKES
4455 Genesee Street
Buffalo, NY 14225
716-626-0400
Fax 716-626-1164

EAST TEXAS
2323 S. Shepherd Street
Houston, TX 77019
713-387-7200
Fax 713-387-7202

GULF
423 Canal Street
New Orleans, LA 70130
504-670-2404
Fax 504-670-2286

MID AMERICA
610 S. Canal Street
Chicago, IL 60607
312-983-9100
Fax 312-886-4921

MID ATLANTIC
103 S. Gay Street
Baltimore, MD 21202
410-962-6200
Fax 410-962-2449

MID PACIFIC
33 New Montgomery Street
San Francisco, CA 94105
415-744-1530
Fax 415-744-7005

NEW YORK
One Penn Plaza, 11th Floor
New York, NY 10119
646-733-3100
Fax 646-733-3245

NORTH ATLANTIC
10 Causeway Street
Boston, MA 02222
617-565-6210
Fax 617-565-6277

NORTH FLORIDA
1624 E. Seventh Avenue
Tampa, FL 33605
813-228-2381
Fax 813-225-7110

NORTH PACIFIC
PO Box 55700
Portland, OR 97238
503-326-7625
Fax 503-326-7629

NORTHWEST GREAT PLAINS
1000 2nd Avenue
Seattle, WA 98104
206-553-4678
Fax 206-553-1401

SOUTH ATLANTIC
1691 Phoenix Boulevard
College Park, GA 30349
770-994-4100
Fax 770-994-4122

SOUTH FLORIDA
909 SE First Avenue
Miami, FL 33131
305-810-5120
Fax 305-810-5143

SOUTH PACIFIC
One World Trade Center
PO Box 32639
Long Beach, CA 90815
562-980-3100
Fax 562-980-3107

SOUTH TEXAS
PO Box 3130
Lincoln-Juarez Bridge
Administrative Building #2
Laredo, TX 78044
956-718-4161
Fax 956-794-1015

SOUTHERN CALIFORNIA
610 W. Ash Street,
Suite 1200
San Diego, CA 92101
619-557-5360
Fax 619-557-5394

WEST GREAT LAKES
613 Abbott Street
Detroit, MI 48226
313-226-2955
Fax 313-226-3118

WEST TEXAS/ NEWMEXICO
9400 Viscount Boulevard
El Paso, TX 79925
915-633-7300
Fax 915-633-7392

SOURCE: U.S. Customs and Border Protection

Glossary

absolute quota A fixed limit on the amount of merchandise that can be imported into a country during a quota period, usually valid for a period of one year

ad valorem tariff A tariff calculated as a percentage of the value of merchandise

African Growth and Opportunity Act (AGOA) An act that offers incentives for African countries in an effort to open economies and build free markets; includes an agreement that apparel made in Sub-Saharan African countries using U.S. fabric, yarn, and thread are duty-free and quota-free

agent A person who acts on behalf of another person. The two types of agents common in international trade are selling agents and buying agents. Selling agents act on behalf of a manufacturer as sales representatives. Buying agents are sales representatives acting on behalf of the buyer, as liaisons between buyer and manufacturer. Agents are paid a commission for their services.

Andean countries (CAN) A South American trade bloc formed in 1997 among member countries Bolivia, Colombia, Ecuador, and Peru. Groundwork for what was originally known as the Andean Pact was laid in 1969 with the signing of the Cartagena Agreement. It is called *Comunidad Andina* in Spanish.

arrival notice An announcement sent by the freight company to the importer to notify him or her of the arrival of goods

assist An importer may provide the manufacturer of export with design work, dies, molds, tools, raw materials, or other forms of aid to produce the product. The importer may not receive payment for the assistance given or may receive payment at less than value. The importer must declare the assist with Customs in his or her country and pay any assessed duty charge in addition to the payment of the cost of merchandise.

Association of Southeast Asian Nations (ASEAN) Association of nations, including Bangladesh, India, Pakistan, Vietnam, Cambodia, Indonesia, Laos, and Sri Lanka

balance of trade The difference between what a country exports and what it imports

bill of lading (B/L) Legal document stating ownership of cargo. The person shipping merchandise is the consignor, the company or agent transporting the goods is the carrier, and the person receiving the product is the consignee.

bond A guarantee issued by an insurance or surety company to assure payment of duty charges in the event the importer is unable to pay

CAN See Andean countries

Caribbean Basin Initiative (CBI) A group of trade programs initially formed with the Caribbean Basin Recovery Act of 1983 (CBERA) to promote economic development in the Caribbean Islands. Benefits include duty-free entry on most goods entering the United States market.

Caribbean Basin Trade Partnership Act (CBTPA) An act signed by President Clinton on October 2, 2000, stating that the 24 Caribbean Basin countries are beneficiary countries with favored tariff treatment. The act proclaims certain items duty-free that previously had duty charges. Apparel made in the Caribbean Basin with fabrics in demand by the United States, and with fabric made in the United States from U.S. yarn, as well as certain Caribbean Basin handmade articles, are now duty- and quota-free.

carriage and insurance paid to (CIP) The buyer indicates the point of destination. The seller delivers the merchandise to the destination indicated on a carrier of his or her choice, obtains insurance for the transportation of goods, and clears for export. The buyer assumes all other costs and responsibility.

carriage paid to (CPT) The buyer indicates the point of destination. The seller delivers the merchandise to the destination indicated on a carrier of his or her choice and clears for export. The buyer assumes all other costs and responsibility.

cash in advance (CIA) Payment of all or a percentage of the total amount due for merchandise prior to shipment of the merchandise

combination tariff Using both specific and ad valorem tariffs to determine the rate of tax on imports

commercial invoice A document prepared by the exporter describing the goods sold, cost of the merchandise, noting country of origin, and itemizing all expenses. A commercial invoice is required to clear Customs.

compound rate A combination of both ad valorem and specific rate. This includes a percentage of the dollar value of the item plus a specified dollar amount based on weight.

consolidated shipment A container with merchandise from more than one shipper

consolidator A shipping company that combines merchandise from more than one factory into one container

cost and freight (CFR) A port of destination is named by the buyer. The seller is responsible to deliver the merchandise "over the rail" of the ship and clears for export. The buyer assumes cost and responsibility for transportation and other costs.

cost, insurance, and freight A port of destination is named by the buyer. The seller is responsible for delivering the merchandise "over the rail" of the ship, pays insurance for the transport, and clears for export. The buyer assumes cost and responsibility for transportation and other costs.

cross-dock order An order produced and imported specifically for a customer that meets FOB requirements, but must be consolidated with the vendor's incoming shipment because it is less than a container load. Upon arrival of the shipment, the customer's merchandise is unloaded without additional handling in the vendor's warehouse and placed at the vendor's dock to ship to the customer. Since the shipment enters the country under the ownership of the vendor, duty and freight is paid by the customer. This is also known as an indirect import (IDI) order.

cultural traits A shared set of values by a group of people acquired and developed over a period of time

customs broker Person or company licensed by the government of the importer that handles entering and clearing of imported merchandise through Customs. A broker prepares the entry form, files the form, advises of duties, may pay the duties in advance, and arranges for transportation of the goods to the purchaser.

customs classification The specific category in the tariff schedule to classify an item for the purpose of determining import taxes and duty. The Harmonized Tariff Schedule is most commonly used.

Customs-Trade Partnership Against Terrorism (C-TPAT) A voluntary partnership agreement between Customs and businesses involved in the supply chain management of importing product. The purpose of C-TPAT is to strengthen security at all stages of importing with the help of importers, carriers, brokers, warehouse operators, and manufacturers. Businesses must apply to Customs and sign the C-TPAT agreement to guarantee the reliability of their security practices. In turn, the members will receive benefits from Customs, such as reduced inspections, access to the list of C-TPAT members, an assigned account manager, and more. C-TPAT membership is open to all importers and carriers.

delivered at frontier (DAF) The seller is responsible for transporting the merchandise to a point (frontier) designated by the buyer and clearing for export. The buyer must clear the merchandise for import, have the goods unloaded, and pay for any additional costs.

delivered duty paid (DDP) This is the maximum obligation for the seller. The seller delivers the merchandise to a destination determined by the buyer and clears goods for both export and import, which includes the payment of any duty owed. The buyer is responsible for unloading the merchandise.

delivered duty unpaid (DDU) The seller delivers the merchandise to a destination determined by the buyer and clears goods for export, but not import. The buyer clears the goods for import and is responsible for unloading the merchandise.

delivered ex quay (DEQ) The seller is responsible for the costs of clearing merchandise for import at the port (quay). After the merchandise has been cleared, the buyer takes ownership.

delivered ex ship (DES) Ownership of imported merchandise is passed from the seller to the buyer on board the ship. The buyer is responsible for the cost of clearing the merchandise for import at the port.

developed countries Countries whose economies are strong as a result of a high level of industrialization

developing countries Countries that are just beginning to become industrialized as they move from a position of under or less developed to a more independent one

direct import order Merchandise ordered for the customer is delivered to the forwarder. Once the product is delivered, the customer takes ownership of the goods and financial responsibility for importing the goods into the United States.

dumping The GATT antidumping code defines dumping as the selling of merchandise at a value lower than normal for goods sold in the exporting country. Dumping is considered an unfair trade practice. GATT Article V allows special antidumping duty charges for merchandise considered dumped. The amount is equal to the difference of the selling price of the goods and the normal value of the goods for the exporting country.

duty Money paid to U.S. Customs for merchandise entering the United States from foreign countries. The dollar amount is calculated by a percentage assigned by U.S. Customs by category.

economic traits The amount of goods and services produced and consumed, as well as the overall state of financial well-being of a country

entry summary A form filed by the Customs agent within 10 days once the shipment is released and estimated duties deposited

estimated landed cost (ELC) The estimated dollar amount to purchase and transport merchandise from the factory to the United States. The calculation is based on FOB price plus duty plus freight.

export Product sold and shipped from a seller in one country to a buyer in another country

ex works (EXW) International commercial trade term that defines the minimal obligation of a seller to deliver merchandise to the buyer from the place of the seller. The buyer assumes responsibility and costs to transport merchandise to a carrier and on to the destination of import.

foreign buying office A buying office located in an overseas country that provides services to help facilitate the importing process for companies that conduct business in that country

foreign trade zone, free trade area Area to receive, warehouse, or modify merchandise without payment of duty until leaving the zone

free alongside ship (FAS) The seller is responsible for delivering merchandise to the ship

free carrier (FCA) The seller delivers merchandise to the carrier and clears for export

FOB (Free on Board) The seller delivers the merchandise "over the rail" of the ship and clears for export

FOB (Free on Board) cost The cost paid to the factory for merchandise. FOB cost does not include duty and freight.

free trade International trade without tariffs or government restrictions

freight consolidator A company that or an individual who sells space in a container and usually combines or consolidates shipments to fill it

freight forwarder A person who or company that books space for shipments on common carriers for the importer or exporter and handles documentation for the shipments

General Agreement on Tariffs and Trade (GATT) An international treaty now superseded by the World Trade Organization (WTO). Agreements still in effect under GATT are the Valuation Code, Antidumping Code, and Subsidies Code.

Generalized System of Preference (GSP) Program developed by the United Nations where quotas and tariffs are eliminated on products imported from less-developed countries

geographical traits Give insight to a buyer into the natural resources that are available in a country

globalization Worldwide trade of merchandise and resources working across borders. Advanced communication technology enables rapid exchange of ideas.

global sourcing Seeking manufacturers or products worldwide

gross domestic product A measurement of goods and services produced by a country in one year

gross national product The value of all goods and services produced by a country in one year. It includes the income generated by domestic and international companies.

GSP Form Certificate of origin of a product that complies with the origin requirements specified in the GSP

Harmonized Tariff Schedule (HTS) Numerical system adopted in 1989 used by most countries to classify merchandise produced and sold internationally

import training seminars Courses offered by a variety of importing experts. Many firms offer assistance and training online.

indirect import order An order produced and imported specifically for a customer and meets FOB requirements, but must be consolidated with the vendor's incoming shipment because it is less than a container load. Upon arrival, the customer's merchandise is unloaded without additional handling in the vendor's warehouse and placed at the vendor's dock to ship to the customer. Since the shipment enters the country under the ownership of the vendor, duty and freight are paid by the customer. See also *cross-dock order*.

inner carton A carton with a predetermined number of units inside a master carton

insurance certificate Formal document that shows the value of goods insured for the cost of cargo, taxes, and duties. It states that the imported goods are covered for certain risks and are presigned for by the insurer.

intermodal bill of lading form Document used if more than one mode of transportation is being used to ship product

international fashion center Building or cluster of buildings that house showrooms representing manufacturers, located throughout the world in major cities such as Paris, Milan, London, New York

International Trade Administration (ITA) An organization designed to assist U.S. businesses participate in international trade

International Trade Commission A U.S. federal agency that maintains the Harmonized Tariff Schedule, protects the United States against unfair trade, and provides industry and economic research

less-developed countries Countries with incomes at poverty level, limited natural resources, unstable political situations, and extremely high unemployment rates.

less-than-container load (LCL) This is when the total cubic feet of the product to be shipped is less than the available cubic feet in the container. The total cost of shipping the merchandise by container is distributed to each unit shipped. If the container is not full, each item will cost more to ship.

letter of credit (LC) A formal document issued by a bank stating its guarantee to pay the seller (exporter) a stated amount of money on behalf of the buyer (importer) as long as the seller meets specific terms and conditions

manifest A document provided by the carrier that lists the cargo to be transported

master carton The shipping carton filled with merchandise ordered by the customer

matchmaker programs Programs sponsored by the Department of Commerce for businesses seeking specific opportunities with businesses with which or persons with whom they may conduct business

minimum order quantity (MOQ) The minimum number of pieces or dollars that a customer is required to order

monochronic Type of culture that organizes single tasks into linear sequences

most favored nation An agreement by one country to give the same or like benefits to another country that the granting country has given to all other countries

Multi-Fiber Agreement (MFA) An agreement negotiated in 1973 that set international quotas on textiles. The quotas defined in the agreement expired on January 1, 2005.

North American Free Trade Agreement (NAFTA) Agreement signed by President George H. W. Bush on December 17, 1992 eliminating trade barriers between Canada, the United States, and Mexico.

Office of Textiles and Apparel (OTEXA) A department that monitors and guides trade-related issues and functions dedicated to the textile and apparel sector

Organization for Economic Cooperation and Development (OECD) In 1961, 25 countries created the OEDC to promote social and economic growth among countries as well as assist them with trade issues

packing list A detailed list of individual items inside one or more cartons of a shipment. Information may include the item number, description, units ordered, cost, weight of items, and freight.

political traits These usually relate to a nation's economy. The political environment of a nation can affect the flow of business daily.

polychronic Type of culture that handles many tasks at the same time

port of entry (POE) order An order produced and imported specifically for a customer in which the customer takes ownership of the container of merchandise at the port of entry agreed upon. The customer pays the duty and freight.

power of attorney form A written document authorizing a person (usually a customs agent) to act as an agent for another person (the importer) as noted in the document

proforma invoice An invoice sent prior to merchandise being transported that lists its value, including estimated weight to determine freight or container space

quota A restriction or limit placed on quantity or duty rate on imported merchandise

royalty An amount or percentage of the value of merchandise paid by a licensee to obtain rights to produce and sell it

social traits The language, education, values, and customs of a group of people

South American Community of Nations Formed from the Cusco Presidential Declaration on December 8, 2004 at the Third South American Presidential Summit. CAN and MERCOSUR member countries merged, along with Guyana and Suriname, to total twelve South American member countries with the common goal to promote a decentralized development program.

specific duty/tariff A tax levied on imported merchandise based on the net weight or number of units rather than value of the item

supply chain management Planning of communications between suppliers and retailers for the purposes of producing and moving merchandise quickly and efficiently

tariff A duty or tax assessed on merchandise that is transported from one customs area to another

tariff rate quota When imported merchandise exceeds the established quota, the tariff rate increases for the amount that merchandise exceeds the quota

trade association Organization of professionals in a specific industry that networks and informs members of all new laws, research, and trade agreements regarding that industry

trade club Organization located in various cities throughout the United States consisting of importers, exporters, custom agents, and freight forwarders who form a network to share information and ideas

trade deficit When a country imports more products than it exports

trade publication Publication for professionals in a specific industry

trade surplus When a country exports more than it imports

United States–Central America–Dominican Republic Free Trade Agreement (CAFTA–DR) This agreement was signed by President George W. Bush on August 5, 2004. It is designed to eliminate trade barriers and tariffs and to expand regional opportunities among the United States, Costa Rica, Dominican Republic, Guatemala, and El Salvador.

United States–Chile Free Trade Agreement (U.S.–CFTA) An agreement signed by George W. Bush on September 3, 2003 and implemented on January 1, 2004, which created duty-free trade for most products between the United States and Chile, with the provision that yarn and fabric must originate in Chile or the United States

United States–Singapore Free Trade Agreement (U.S.–SFTA) This is the first free-trade agreement signed with an Asian country, as well as the first free-trade agreement signed by President George W. Bush. The agreement was finalized on January 15, 2003 and guarantees no duty on U.S. merchandise and duty on Singapore imports to be phased out within a 10-year period.

valuation The determination of the value of imported merchandise by Customs to decide the amount of ad valorum duty. The value is generally the price paid by the seller for the merchandise.

wire transfer Electronic transfer of funds from buyer's bank to seller's bank to pay for merchandise or service

World Trade Organization (WTO) Global international organization that replaced GATT in January 1995, which had a membership of 148 countries as of February 2005. The organization deals with trade issues among countries through collective negotiations to support commerce among manufacturers, importers, and exporters.

Bibliography

Abernathy, F. and D. Weiss (2004, November 17) "Apparel Apocalypse?" *Washington Post,* Page A 39. [Online] Available: www.washingtonpost.com/wp-dym/articles/A58831-2004Nov17.html.

Baker, S. (2004). "Next Trends in Apparel Retail, Manufacturing, Fashion and Merchandising." just-style.com.[Online] Available: www.just-style.com.

Crutsinger, M. (2005, April 3). "Imports May Threaten U.S. Textile Jobs." *Associated Press.* [Online]. Available: ap.org.home.

EmergingTextiles.com (2005, March 21) "U.S. Imports of Cotton Denim Trousers in January 2005" (Statistical Report). [Online] Available: EmergingTextiles.com

Flanagan, M. (2003, January). "Apparel Sourcing in the 21st Century, The 10 Lessons So Far." Just-style.com.

Gresser, E. (2004). "The Big Bang: Ending Quota and Tariff Policies." American Apparel and Footwear Association. [Online] Available: http://www.apparelandfootwear.org/data/2005assnreportbig-bang040105.pdf.

Guthrie, K. M. and C. W. Pierce (2003). *Perry's Department Store: A Buying Simulation for Juniors, Men's Wear, Children's Wear, and Home Fashion/Giftware* (2nd ed.). New York: Fairchild Publications, Inc.

Hodge, S. (2000). *Global Smarts* (1st ed.), New York: John Wiley & Sons Inc.

Johnson, T. (2002). *Export/Import Procedures and Documentation.* (4th ed.), New York: AMACOM.

Just-style.com (2004, August 23). "2005: The Real Uncertainty." [Online] Available: www.just-style.com.

Keiser, Sandra J. and Myrna B. Garner (2003) *Beyond Design: The Synergy of Apparel Product Development.* New York: Fairchild Publications, Inc.

Marshall, J. (2004, August 29). "Migrating Southward." *The Free Lance-Star.* [Online]. Available: www.fredericksburg.com

Morrissey, James A. (2005, February) "Textile and Apparel Imports Rose in 2004." *Textile World.* [Online] Available: www.textileworld.com

Nelson, Carl A. (2000). *Import Export: How to Get Started in International Trade.* New York: McGraw-Hill.

NETD Merchants Bureau. *Investment Guide: Ningbo Economic & Technical Development Zone.* Edited by: NETD Merchants Bureau, Beilun, Ningbo.

"Our Policies to Promote a Fair and Just Workplace." (2003) Liz Claiborne Inc. [Online] Available: www.lizclaiborneinc.com/rights/conduct.asp.

Pekar, F. (2004). "Keeping Abreast of Customs Rules." *Apparel.* [Online] Available: http://www.bobbin.com/bobbin/headlines.

Ryan, T. (2003). "Sourcing: The Need for Speed, Global Logistics, Sourcing Systems and Remote Factory Floor-ready Preparation are Among Key Focus Areas for Apparel Importers as They Strive to Reduce Cycle Time." *Apparel,* 44 (6).

Stone, E. (2004). *The Dynamics of Fashion* (2nd ed.). New York: Fairchild Publications, Inc.

Textile World. (2005, March). "Quota-free Imports from China Reach Record Levels." [Online] Available: www.TextileWorld.com.

Tyagi, R. (2003, January 1). "Apparel Globalization: The Big Picture." *Apparel*. [Online] Available: http://www.bobbin.com/bobbin.

"Trading Into the Future." (2001). [Online] Available: http://www.wto.org.

U.S. Customs and Border Protection. (2004, November). "Becoming a Broker and Maintaining a License and Contact Information." [Online]. Available: www.CBP.gov.

————. (2004, November). "Import Specialist." [Online] Available: www.CBP.gov.

U.S. Customs Service. (2002). *Importing Into the United States: A Guide for Commercial Importers*. Washington, D.C.: U.S. Customs Service.

U.S. Census Bureau. (2005, February 1). Virginia QuickFacts. [Online] Available: www.census.gov.

Weiss, K. (2002). *Building an Import/Export Business* (3rd ed.). New York: John Wiley & Sons, Inc.

Yousaf, N. (2001). *Import and Export of Apparel and Textiles* (1st ed.). Liverpool, N.Y.: Author.

Index